They Call Us to Justice

Responding to the Call of the Church and Our Students

Mark G. Storz & Karen R. Nestor

© 2007 National Catholic Educational Association

1077 30th Street, NW, Suite 100

Washington, DC 20007–3852

ISBN: 1-55833-398-3

Part No.: SDV–22–1390

Table of Contents

Introduction vii

Chapter 1   Who is Calling Us to Justice? 1

The Students' Voices..*2*

The Church's Voice: Catholic Social Teaching...*5*

Catholic Social Teaching at a Glance...*7*

Organization of the Book...*12*

Chapter 2   They Call Us to Respect the Dignity of the Human Person 15

What does the Church mean by the dignity of the human person? ..17

What do students tell us about the dignity of the human person? ...19

It's all about caring *20*

High Expectations *32*

Effective Teaching and Learning *39*

*How do we judge our response to the call to respect the dignity
of the human person?* *52*

Discussion *53*

Chapter 3   They Call Us to Community 55

What does the Church mean by community? 58

What do students tell us about community? 63

It's (still) all about caring 63

We are Family 68

Students and Teachers in Classrooms 69

Faculty Relationships 74

Family-School Relationships 76

Really Knowing Each Other 80

Personal Responsibility and Community 85

Our Responsibility as Teachers 88

The Value of Service: How do we judge our response to the call
to community? 90

Discussion 91

Chapter 4   They Call us to a Preferential Option for the Poor & Vulnerable 93

What does the Church mean by a Preferential Option for the
Poor & Vulnerable? 96

What do students tell us about a Preferential Option for the
Poor & Vulnerable? 100

Academic Issues – Curriculum and Expectations 104

Teacher Characteristics 107

Lack of Resources 110

Examining Assumptions 114

How do we judge our response to the call to a preferential option
for the poor & vulnerable? 121

Discussion 123

Chapter 5   They Call Us to Act 127

Listening to Our Students 130

Teacher Collaboration 133

Class Meetings & Other School Rituals 136

Curriculum & Instruction 138

Service Learning 141

Collaboration with Families 144

Action Research 148

Appendix A: Seven Themes of Catholic Social Teaching 157

Appendix B: Selected Quotations from Scripture and Church Documents 161

Resources for Further Reflection 169

About the Authors 187

Introduction

" Listen to the kids. People say kids don't know any-
thing, but kids do know more than adults think. So I
think you should ask the kids because they do know
more than you think they know."

—*Ricardo, Eighth-Grade student*

Wᴴᴱɴ ʏᴏᴜ ᴘɪᴄᴋᴇᴅ ᴜᴘ ᴛʜɪꜱ ʙᴏᴏᴋ, ᴡᴇ ꜱᴜꜱᴘᴇᴄᴛ ᴛʜᴀᴛ ᴛʜᴇ ꜰɪʀꜱᴛ question you asked yourself was: *"Who are THEY and what do THEY have to do with justice?"* No self-respecting teacher could fail to ask what the antecedent is for that pronoun THEY. And the answer to that question is at the very heart of our purpose in writing this book. As Catholic educators, we hear frequent calls to incorporate justice teaching into our work. Often these calls come to us in the form of mandates from the diocese or from our principals. Usually these mandates come to the forefront as we prepare documents for accrediting our schools or when we are designing lesson plans or service projects that incorporate social justice in some way. But we all know on some level that our call is more personal and more compelling than any mandate. What voices are actually calling us to our most profound work in schools?

Four years ago, we began an unexpected journey that reinvigorated our lives as Catholic educators. We were both teacher educators doing our best to make a difference in classrooms in our city. We started on a small project that we thought might help teachers improve their practice. It was nothing exciting, just an exercise in studying what was happening in a few classrooms. Little by little, the students in those classrooms transformed our teaching lives and we reconnected with the vocation or call we had experienced many years ago when we became Catholic educators.

The story began when a group of teachers from a kindergarten through grade 8 school came to us with a simple request: *"We want our school to become a better place for students to learn. Would you help us?"* That small group of concerned teachers met with us on their own time during the summer to analyze the problems they observed in their school. Initially the focus was on the behavior of the students. Their major question was: *"How can we get our students to behave better so that they will learn better?"* They wanted to create a behavior plan that would ensure that things would go well in the new school year. While behavior was an important issue for these teachers to address, we decided to shift the conversation slightly to engage the group in what they already knew about child development and the cultural heritage of the students in the school. Slowly this group began to believe that real solutions might require more than highly structured rules and consequences; rather that effective teaching and learning might be the key to good behavior *and* to students' academic success. In effect, these teachers had made a commitment to justice: they recognized that unfair or ineffective practices in their school hindered student achievement and they set themselves on a course of action to enhance their own knowledge and skills to address that unfairness. In retrospect the teachers illustrated for us the clear connection between sound pedagogy and social justice. If we truly are committed to social justice, the place to begin as teachers is in providing our students with rich and meaningful learning experiences in a caring and nurturing environment.

At the end of the summer, the teachers convinced a few more colleagues to join regular meetings with us to explore attitudes and practices that might improve teaching and learning. Often attempts to discuss ideas or to implement best practices were met with opposition because of teachers' feelings of frustration, anger, and even hopelessness about prospects for improvement. Many teachers had come to believe that no matter what they did or what best practices they employed, it would not work with many of their own students.

Quite frankly we were discouraged at our own inability to help the teachers look at things in new ways. As we tried to create alternative means to build dialogue with the teachers, we thought it might be helpful for them to hear what their own students had to say about their schooling. In small focus groups, we asked students in these classrooms about their academic experiences and the quality of the relationships in their schools. Their responses to our questions were profound and insightful and we used the students' responses to help ourselves and the teachers reflect more deeply on our professional practice. It was this experience that served as a catalyst for a research project that extended over two years and led us to interview almost three hundred urban young adolescents.

In our work with teachers we have found that when teachers actually listen to the voices of their students, many experience dramatic changes in their perceptions, attitudes, and assessment of their teaching practice. Perhaps the best example of this type of change came when we presented the students' conversations to a group of middle school teachers and asked them to comment on what they had heard. A mid-career teacher was visibly moved when she said: *"Remember when the students said that their teacher compared them to Chinese people – and it made them feel bad? That teacher was me. I never thought about what I was saying from their point of view. I thought that I was motivating them. Oh, my gosh – I just never looked at it like that."* That teacher had heard her students' voices as she never had before and it had a powerful effect on her. She went on to take several graduate courses in urban education in order to change her classroom practice to serve her students better.

We ourselves were stunned by what we learned from the students we interviewed. When we began to listen carefully to the profound things the students told us, we were reminded of our own Catholic faith tradition and the church's longstanding commitment to social justice. While our original interviews were done in a public school setting, we heard echoes of the work we had done in Catholic schools for many years and began to realize that what these students were saying held significant implications for Catholic education. We shared our interviews with Catholic school teachers at the NCEA convention and they heard in those voices the same issues that were both opportunities and barriers to success for their own students. Eventually we interviewed students in Catholic schools and they raised many of the same issues as their public school peers. Most importantly, we began to consider the mandate of the Catholic Bishops that: *"Catholic teaching proclaims that a basic moral test is how our most vulnerable members are faring."*

As we discussed these ideas with more and more teachers, we realized that the students had led us to a new way of considering our vocation as Catholic educators and our work in Catholic schools. We have known for a long time that the Church was calling us to bring Catholic Social Teaching into our schools, but it was not until the voices of students joined the voice of the Church that we recognized the depth and breadth of the true call we were hearing. Without knowing it, students introduced us to profound ways of looking at our work with them. The students' words challenged us to deepen our knowledge and understanding of Catholic social teaching and to engage in cycles of reflection as Catholic educators committed to justice. It is our work with these students that provides the foundation for this book.

Individual formation and change comes most readily when teachers, like those who first came to us for help, engage in ongoing dialogue around these important issues. When teachers share their beliefs and questions with each other, they can gradually extend their understanding to changes in attitudes and practices throughout the school. We invite you to join us in creating just such a process of discovery about vocation, schooling, and social justice – by yourself, with a few colleagues, or in a school-wide dialogue. We hope that the students will lead you, too, to discover anew your passion for teaching in Catholic schools, of teaching from a deep commitment to the social justice that is at the core of our faith tradition.

CHAPTER ONE

─◦◦◦◦─

Who is Calling Us to Justice?

" *Our faith calls us to work for justice; to serve those in need; to pursue peace and to defend the life, dignity and rights of all our sisters and brothers. This is the call of Jesus, the challenge of the prophets and the living tradition of the Church.*"

—*USCCB, 1997, p. 37*

MANY OF US CAME TO TEACHING BECAUSE WE BELIEVED WE were called to teach. Particularly in Catholic education, we see teaching as a vocation, a call from God to serve through our work with children and adults. No doubt each of us has our own story about how we came to the profession and the reasons why we responded to God's call. We sometimes wonder if we fully understood the significance of being called at the time we began our teacher preparation program or entered our first classroom at the beginning of our career. We may look back and wonder what was God really calling me to? And why did God choose me? Answers to these questions are personal and will vary for each of us, but whatever our story, we believe that in calling us, God uses the voices of our students and the Church to help us minister faithfully as Catholic educators. And we believe that if we truly listen to these voices, we will realize that what we are being called to is justice – responding to the students and to the Church in such a way that we transform our practice into a full response to the Gospel message of love. In order to really listen to these voices we need to be aware of who is speaking to us, who is calling us in our vocation as Catholic educators. In this chapter we will describe these voices that call us every day to be just in our vocation as Catholic educators.

The Students' Voices

We think that teachers would universally agree that the focus of our work, the reason we respond to that call to teach, is the students who are entrusted to our care one hundred and eighty days each year. Our research has shown us that students have profound insights into their educational experiences, particularly into the types of teachers and pedagogical practices that help them achieve success in school. It has also shown us that, when given the opportunity, students are ready and willing to share their insights with us, at times giving us more information than we even want! Who are these students we will present to you throughout this book? How have they touched our lives and our work? Who are the students who attend our nation's Catholic schools? And who are the students you encounter on a daily basis?

The students we interviewed for our research project attended various public and parochial schools in a large mid-western metropolitan area. They came from public middle schools, and K-8 schools that were part of a large urban public school district. Some students came from a middle school located in a smaller suburban area. Other students came from a number of parochial schools, all of which were located in the urban center of the diocese. Our students were African-American, White, and Hispanic. They ranged in age from eleven to fourteen. They came from a variety of income levels. Some were outgoing; some were shy. Some loved school and were engaged in their learning, while others seemed to lack motivation and interest in school. There were academically gifted students, academically-challenged students, and everyone else in-between. There were 'wise guys' and there were angels. There were philosophers and there were sports stars. Some were on the honor roll while others were failing nearly every class. Some made us laugh and others literally made us cry. In all, we interviewed almost 300 randomly selected sixth, seventh, and eighth-grade students. When we asked, teachers at the schools reported that the students represented a cross section of personalities and ability levels, providing us with what we think is a balanced perspective of these students' experiences, ideas, and beliefs about their education. Their responses to our questions were amazingly consistent no matter what the setting or the varied characteristics of each of the students.

The students we talked with, while not all parochial school students, were similar to the students who attend our nation's Catholic schools. According to data provided by the National Catholic Educational Association in the *Annual Report on Catholic Schools, 2005-2006* (McDonald,

2006), students attending today's Catholic schools are a varied group of young people. Of the 2,363,220 students enrolled in 7,589 schools across our country, 27.1% are minority students. In some of our urban centers, the percentage is higher (e.g., Washington D.C. is 45% minority; in Chicago 38% of its students are minority). Over 43% of all Catholic schools are located in urban areas, while 35.2% and 21.6% are in suburban and rural areas, respectively. Given the numbers, we would suggest that the students we spoke with, particularly given the consistency of their remarks across school settings, do reflect the experiences of many of the students who attend our schools. As a result, we believe that the insights of the students we interviewed provide all of us with a realistic picture of life in many of our schools, insights we will be able to use as we reflect on our practice throughout this book.

As you look around your own classroom and school, we are certain that you see students like the ones we interviewed, who are similar to those in other Catholic schools around the country. You are no doubt keenly aware of the intense variety of the ability levels, special needs, developmental stages, and personalities of your students. Add to this the different ethnic groups and income levels and you have quite an array of young people. In addition, even within groups that appear rather homogeneous, there can be great variety. How this diversity impacts students' experiences and our ability to effectively teach and interact with them can be a complex, and even daunting challenge. We think this is why listening carefully to our students can make a difference. We hope to illustrate in the following chapters how insights provided by students can be a powerful and enlightening opportunity for us to respond to our call to be teachers. As a side note we want to mention that when you read the students' quotations and conversations you will notice that we have not substantially edited their words as a way of honoring their voices and their ideas. All of the names that are used are pseudonyms.

At times in the text we have quoted teachers as well. These were teachers the students identified as the ones who helped them succeed in school.

Some were veteran teachers and some were novices. They taught a variety of grades and disciplines. We interviewed them and asked them to talk about what made them effective with their students. We include their voices as a way of confirming what the students told us about quality education. We were struck by how the ideas of the teachers matched those of the students in defining good practice in schools.

The Church's Voice: Catholic Social Teaching

Early in our interviews with students we met a young man named Jamal. Jamal was a seventh grader who appeared to us to be a "typical" middle school student (whatever that might be!) and who was fully engaged in his education. One of the stunning things he shared with us while speaking about his perspectives on education was: *"How will I learn without knowing my history?"* We encountered another young man later in our project, who, like Jamal, loved history. Michael was about to enter ninth-grade when we spoke with him about his schooling experiences. He told us emphatically: *"If you don't know about your history, you got no future."* In the context of these conversations, it was clear that both Jamal and Michael were eager to learn about things that were relevant to their real world experiences as young urban adolescents and their cultural heritage as African-Americans. These young men had a thirst for learning and an understanding of the important role history plays in their lives. We use the insights of Jamal and Michael to introduce Catholic social teaching because the social mission it defines is such a vital and central part of the history of the Church and the tradition that calls us to be Catholic educators. The U.S. Bishops' 1998 statement entitled: *Sharing Catholic Social Teaching: Challenges and Directions*, focuses on both the historical and contemporary significance of Catholic social teaching in the life of the Church, particularly as it impacts the educational mission of the Church. In their statement, the bishops present a concern and a challenge, acknowledging the fact that: *"far too many Catholics are not familiar with*

the basic content of Catholic Social Teaching" (1998, p. 3). A task force*
commissioned by the U. S. Bishops to assess current efforts for sharing
this body of teaching concluded that while:

> *There is much interest among Catholic educational, catechetical,*
> *and social ministry professionals to incorporate Catholic social*
> *teaching into Catholic Educational programs . . . the extent to which*
> *it actually happens is very uneven and is often lacking depth and*
> *clarity. (USCCB, 1998, p. 12)*

As an essential part of our faith, the history of the Church and its educational mission, Catholic social teaching is at the core of what it means to be
Catholic in the world today. It provides the catalyst and the direction for
our commitment to social justice. The bishops have stated that the teachings that define the social mission of the Church are not optional or on the
fringe, but rather are fundamental to Catholic education and catechesis.
The bishops go so far as to assert: *"If Catholic education and formation fail*
to communicate our social tradition, they are not fully Catholic" (USCCB,
1998, p.2). Both Jamal and Michael can offer us insights here. If teachers are
to be fully engaged in their vocation as Catholic educators, they need to
know "their history": the tradition that calls us to a commitment to justice
that defines our work with students and their families. If we are to integrate
Catholic social teaching into our work, it becomes our responsibility as
Catholic educators to deepen our understanding of this body of teaching
(individually and together), living its precepts in our interactions with students, colleagues and parents. This dimension of our ongoing faith formation provides us the credibility and the solid grounding necessary to be
thoughtful in examining our practice and skillful in sharing this rich tradition with those with whom we are called to serve. Without it, our work is
hollow. Let's begin with a brief discussion of what exactly the Church is
calling us to through its social teaching.

---

* In 1995 the U. S. Bishops' Conference established the Task Force on Catholic Social Teaching and Catholic
Education to examine the extent to which Catholic social teaching was being taught and to develop innova-
tions for future implementation. Final results of the task force's work were reported in January 1998.

Catholic Social Teaching at a Glance

Catholic social teaching has been referred to as the *"Church's best kept secret,"* (DeBerri & Hug, 2003), because Catholics tend to be less familiar with its content than that of other moral issues on which the Church has taken a position. DeBerri and Hug (2003) underscore this fact when they suggest:

> *That the Church has a developed body of teaching on social, economic, political, and cultural matters and what that body says seem to have been forgotten – or have never been known – by a majority of the Roman Catholic community in the United States. (p. 3)*

Yet our Judeo-Christian tradition has called us to justice from the very beginning through the voices of the Hebrew prophets, Jesus and his disciples, the saints, popes, bishops, and lay men and women. Catholic social teaching, an integral part of Catholic identity, provides the foundation of the Church's commitment to social justice and its teachings on the human person and the human community. According to the Task Force on Catholic Social Teaching and Catholic Education (1998), the call to justice is:

> *Founded in the life and words of Jesus Christ . . . inspired by the passion for justice in the Hebrew prophets . . . articulated by the social teachings of our Church . . . shaped by those who have come before us . . . lived by the People of God. (pp. 22-23)*

Catholic social teaching is not only a doctrine, but also a blueprint for action. It promotes the sanctity and dignity of the human person and the idea that the good of each individual is inextricably linked with the good of the community (Curran, 2002). First recognized by Pope Leo XIII, in his encyclical *Rerum Novarum* (1891), Catholic social teaching comes to us from popes and bishops who have responded to the call of the Scriptures and have articulated the Church's commitment to social justice. Initially, their writings focused almost exclusively on economic realities brought about by the Industrial Revolution. Pope John XXIII and his successors, however, provided a more comprehensive response to the various types of injustices that have continued to plague societies around the globe. They promoted *"social justice for all,"* not only in the economic sphere, but in the political, social, and cultural realms as well.

Catholic social teaching is an evolving body of principles which are refined as the Church considers events that affect our world at any given moment in history (*Catechism of the Catholic Church, 2000*). These teachings cover a wide range of subjects that are so important in our own time: poverty and wealth, unemployment, labor issues, war and peace, the arms race, family, health care, racism, prejudice, cultural pluralism, and environmental and ecological issues (NCCB, 1991). Catholic social teaching provides each of us the tools necessary to reflect on the injustices that plague humanity and to act to correct them (*Catechism of the Catholic Church, 2000*); in the words of the U. S. Catholic Bishops: *"it* [Catholic social teaching] *is believers advocating in the public arena for human life wherever it is threatened"* (NCCB, 1991, p.1).

Catholic social teaching does not, however, explicitly address education in the same manner that it confronts other economic, social, political and cultural issues. This is not to say that Catholic social teaching has ignored education. Over the years, the popes have argued that humans have an inherent basic human right to an education (see for example *Pacem in Terris* (1963) and *Guadium et Spes* (1966). More recently, Pope John Paul II has reminded Catholics that in order for the Church to spread the Gospel, Catholic social teaching must concern itself with basic human rights, including the right to education (*Centesimus Annus,* (1991). In *Justice in the World* (Second General Assembly of the Synod of Bishops, 1971), the world's bishops confirmed that education plays a vital role in bringing about the gospel message of justice. The bishops stated that education for justice needs to be of concern to *"every person of every age."* In addition, they made it clear that *"goodwill is not enough."* Education for justice requires Catholic educators to commit to action in order to bring about the change necessary to eradicate injustice.

The U.S. Bishops have been a strong voice as they have addressed education in a number of their writings. In 1968, the National Conference of

Catholic Bishops declared that the educational opportunities available to the poor in this country are: *"pitifully inadequate,"* *"a moral imperative,"* and a crisis *"of a magnitude and peril far transcending any which the Church in America or the nation has previously confronted."* In a 1986 letter entitled: *Building Peace: A Pastoral Reflection on the Response to 'The Challenges of Peace,* the Bishops recognized the inadequacy of the educational system for urban students, supporting public policy for guaranteeing the right of an *"adequate education"* for urban youth. In fact, Catholic social teaching calls into question the very economic, political, social and cultural systems that govern and influence education.

In an effort to simplify and make more readable this large and complex body of teaching that to this point has defined the social mission of the Church, the U.S. Catholic Bishops in *Sharing Catholic Social Teaching: Challenges and Directions* (1998) put forward seven themes (see Appendix A) that are widely used to synthesize Catholic social teaching. This framework provides us easier access to this vast body of teaching in order to facilitate understanding of its essential elements. Based on our study of Catholic social teaching, we have chosen to group these various themes into three central ideas which for us speak to the essence of Catholic social teaching as it relates to what the students told us about their schooling experiences and to our role as Catholic educators:

- The Dignity of the Human Person;

- The Primacy of Community; and

- The Preferential Option for the Poor and Vulnerable

These three ideas, or bedrock principles, encompass many of the important concepts embedded in the themes articulated by the bishops and provide us with a framework for the way Catholic social teaching can be directly related to the school context and our work as Catholic educators. According to the U.S. Catholic Bishops (1998), human dignity is: *"the foundation of all the principles of our social teaching"* (p. 4) as well as *"the foundation of a moral vision of society"* (p. 4). Likewise, the dignity of each of the children we serve is at the very core of our vocation as Catholic educators. The bishops stated: *"how we organize society . . . directly affects human dignity and the capacity of individuals to grow in community"* (1998, p.4). Similarly, the learning environments we create in our schools, classrooms, and in our personal interactions with students can respect or diminish students' dignity while at the same time profoundly impacting their growth and development. Finally, the bishops instruct the faithful that: *"a basic moral test is how our most vulnerable members are faring"* (1998, p.5). A healthy community requires that the needs of all its members are met, particularly those with the greatest need, thus calling for a preferential option for the poor and vulnerable. In schools we have students who, for a variety of reasons, are in particular need, and how we address those needs determines the extent to which we are teaching for equity and justice.

As we read and re-read and analyzed what we heard from the students we interviewed, we saw that these three principles (dignity, community, and equity) also provided us a new way of thinking about and capturing what we were hearing from them and how their words and experiences might help us to examine our practice as Catholic educators. We were profoundly moved when these students described how their experiences in schools promoted and threatened their dignity as human persons. They helped to remind us of the importance of caring relationships, personal responsibility, and commitment that are necessary for developing a healthy human person and a nurturing community in which individuals can grow and develop to meet their God-given potential. Many of these young adolescents also understood the inequities that plague their schools and that compromise their dignity and obstruct their opportunity to take advantage of what society has to offer them. They alerted us to the fact that many of our young people, particularly those with the greatest need, are painfully aware that they are not faring well in the current climate. In short, in synthesizing the mandate of the Church and the experiences of the children, we have come to see a direct connection between Catholic educators' commitment to justice and the quality of the interactions and pedagogy that are present in their classrooms and schools.

One of our goals in writing this book is to respond to the U.S. Bishops' concern and challenge regarding our understanding of Catholic social teaching. We hope that by discussing the three bedrock principles introduced earlier in this chapter, this book will help Catholic educators like you become more familiar with fundamental aspects of Catholic social teaching, particularly as they relate to our work in schools.

A second goal, intimately related to the first, is to provide you an opportunity to reflect on your own practice as an educator committed to the social justice mission of the Church, and to do so by listening to the voices of the Church and to those of students like your own as they share their perspectives on education. In other words, we want to explore what it means to be a Catholic educator committed to justice, a justice demanded by Scripture and the Church, and by the students we teach. Put another way, how do I (individually and collectively, with other members of my school community), embody the social teachings of the Church in my pedagogy and in my interactions with students?

We have a third goal related to the students who participated in our research. Early on in our work we came across an article that cautioned those of us who seek to privilege students' experiences, beliefs, and critiques in educational research (like we are doing in this book) not to relegate the students' voice to: *"an end in itself – a celebration after which we return to the everyday"* (Smith, as cited in Brooks & MacDonald, 1999, p. 86). We agree that to use student voice in this way undermines the spirit and intent of this line of inquiry and continues to marginalize the students. If we are to value the students' experiences and involve them in educational reform efforts, we need to find ways to bring their voices to the fore. This book offers us the opportunity to share with you what we heard from urban young adolescents. We hope that by listening to the voices of these students you might be inspired to listen to the voices of your own students more closely. And we hope that by listening to the students and to the teachings of the Church, we might all look more deeply into our hearts and minds and into our practice as we continually respond to their call to justice.

Implicit in all of this is a call to action. John XXIII in his encyclical, Mater et Magistra (1961), wrote:

"It is not enough merely to formulate a social doctrine. It must be translated into reality. And this is particularly true of the Church's social doctrine, the light of which is Truth, Justice its objective, and Love its driving force (226)."

As Catholic educators, it should not be sufficient simply to reflect on the social teaching of the Church and on the experiences of our students as we strive to teach for justice. And so a fourth goal for writing this book is to stimulate Catholic educators to respond to the call by the Church and by our students to turn our reflection into action.

Organization of the Book

In the next three chapters we will explore in more depth the three principles outlined above: the dignity of the human person, the primacy of community, and the preferential option for the poor and vulnerable. In each chapter we shall begin with a section on what we perceive the Church to mean by each of the three principles. Based on our reading of Scripture, church documents, and scholars in the field, we shall provide a discussion of the three principles, particularly in terms of how they might be related to our work as Catholic educators. Following this section, we shall turn to the voices of the students we interviewed to help illuminate how these principles are reflected in our work in schools. The voices of the students, we believe, will help us understand these bedrock principles of Catholic social teaching and how they relate to our practice.

To help us reflect on the students' experiences and the social teaching of the Church, we will provide questions for reflection in each of the chapters that are based on a framework provided by Pope John XXIII. In his writings, the pope provided a process for translating thought into practice. He instructed us:

"First, one reviews the concrete situation; secondly, one forms a judgment on it in the light of these same principles; thirdly, one decides what in the circumstances can and should be done to implement these principles. These are the three stages that are usually expressed in the three terms: observe, judge, act.

(Mater et Magistra, 1961, #236)

We will adapt this process proposed by John XXIII, namely: *"observe, judge, act,"* as a framework for reflecting and acting on our vocation as teachers. In the body of these three chapters we will provide questions that will ask you to 'observe' your practice as you listen to the students' voices and those of the Church. At the end of each of the chapters, we shall pose questions for individual and collective reflection that will help us to 'judge' or evaluate our practice.

In Chapter 5, we shall respond to John XXIII's call to act in the third step of his framework. This chapter will provide some ideas that we believe may assist Catholic educators who are interested in transforming their practice, individually and collaboratively, in light of Catholic social teaching and the insights gained by listening to the experiences of students.

CHAPTER TWO

They Call Us to Respect the Dignity of the Human Person

" . . . the Catholic Church proclaims that human life is sacred and that the dignity of the human person is the foundation of a moral vision for society. Our belief in the sanctity of human life and the inherent dignity of the human person is the foundation of all the principles of our social teaching."

—USCCB, 1998, p. 4

SHERONDA, A NINTH-GRADE STUDENT COMMITTED TO JUSTICE, defined social justice for us when she said: *"Social justice is your basic human dignity."* Just as the United States bishops have placed the life and dignity of the human person as the first theme in their document, *Sharing Catholic Social Teaching: Challenges and Directions* (USCCB, 1998), Sheronda reminded us that unless we as teachers exercise respect for human dignity, we cannot be just. This may sound like an obvious point – of course, we all respect our students. That is a given for teachers, especially in Catholic schools. But when we listened to students' very strong feelings about their experiences of respect in their school life, we recognized our need to examine in much more concrete ways our own rather rote notions of respect for life and the dignity of the human person

When we first began to interview students, justice was nowhere on our radar screen. We wanted to know what worked, specifically what teaching strategies students found helpful to their learning. After all, we started doing this work as a way to assist a team of teachers, and teachers being who we are, like to get information that is practical and useful and that can be taken back to our classrooms and used the next day. But the students surprised us, they challenged us, they stretched us to see beyond the technical aspects of our work – they called us to see how justice is integral to every aspect of teaching and learning and to their success in school. When we finally heard this call from the students, it caused us to think about the Church's mandate to respect the life and dignity of every person.

Little by little, we began to see that when students talked about their learning, they not only talked about the content and techniques their teachers used, but also looked well beyond these to the underlying relationships and structures that support them as learners. We began to hear students like Tameka in a new way when she said: *"To get a good education, you need teachers that care and students that care. Teachers that care about their students, and the students, they care about themselves."* We realized that Tameka was not simply telling us what teaching techniques worked for her, she was alerting us to principles that form the very foundation of our work in schools, most importantly the fundamental life and dignity of the human person. Tameka and so many other students shared with us that their school experiences at times enhanced their dignity as human persons and at times diminished their dignity. They led us to go back and re-examine the Church's teaching on the dignity of the human person as it relates to Catholic education.

What does the Church mean by the dignity of the human person?

" We believe that every person is precious, that people are more important than things, and that the measure of every institution is whether it threatens or enhances the life and dignity of the human person."

—*USCCB, 1998, p. 4*

One of our earliest childhood lessons is that we are made in God's likeness. The first chapter of Genesis tells us: *"God created man in his own image, in the image of God he created him; male and female he created them"* (Genesis 1:27). This idea is so basic to our understanding of ourselves that it often goes unexamined in practical ways. What difference does this belief make in our daily interactions with others at home, at school, in the world? The U.S. bishops urge us to think more deeply when they say:

> *"The human person is the clearest reflection of God's presence in the world; all of the Church's work in pursuit of both justice and peace is designed to protect and promote the dignity of every person. For each person not only reflects God, but is the expression of God's creative*

work and the meaning of Christ's redemptive ministry." (The Challenge of Peace, 1983, #15)

Like all of our fellow Catholic educators, we have been motivated by this belief that our students are God's own children. Pope John XXIII wrote: *"The permanent validity of the Catholic Church's social teaching admits no doubt. This teaching rests on one basic principle: individual human beings are the foundation, the cause, and the end of every social institution"* (Mater et Magistra, 1961). Schools, of course, are one of the most basic social institutions in our world, and Pope John left no doubt as to the notion that we must focus on every individual as the *"foundation, cause, and end"* of our work in the classroom. Pope John Paul II emphasized that this notion applies equally to young children when he wrote: *". . . special attention must be devoted to children by developing a profound esteem for their personal dignity, and a great respect and generous concern for their rights. . . .it becomes all the more urgent the smaller the child is. . . .:* (Familiaris Consortio, #26).

The Catechism of the Catholic Church (2000) reminds us that: *"being in the image of God, the human individual possesses the dignity of a person, who is not just something, but someone. . . .capable of self-knowledge, or self-possession"* (#357). In the *New Testament,* Jesus reached out time after time to those who received the least respect from society: the disabled, the sinner, and the socially inept. He referred frequently to the dignity of the marginalized as when he said: *". . .the one who is the least among all of you, this is the one who is great"* (Luke 9:48). Jesus did not let the Apostles off with a general love for their fellow human beings; he often pointed out the ones who were annoying and challenged his friends to change their own behavior.

Observe ✍

It might be helpful to stop here and reflect on the children who seem to "deserve" the least respect in my classroom. Which children are marginalized in one way or another? Which children might need very different responses from me than the group in general?

The Church's teaching on the dignity of the human person is clear about the ways in which the individual should be valued. The most important consideration is that the dignity of the individual is more important than the needs of institutions. As John XXIII wrote: *"Any human society, if it is to be well-ordered and productive, must lay down as a foundation this principle, namely that every human being is a person [whose] nature is endowed with intelligence and free will"* (Pacem in Terris, 1963, #9). Schools are institutions that require order for them to succeed, but the Church's teaching reminds us that, to be effective, order must be grounded in each individual's exercise of intellect and choice. Sometimes this seems unrealistic to those of us who work with children (we all have stories of children who refused to *"go along with the program"*), but the Church and the students we interviewed assert that such grounding is the only way to create an environment that supports the development of each individual and the overall success of the classroom.

Observe

Are there aspects of the Church's teaching on the life and dignity of the human person that are new to you? Can you see this theme of social justice in new ways that apply to your work as a Catholic educator?

What do students tell us about the dignity of the human person?

As we consider the way(s) the dignity of the human person relates directly to our work in classrooms, we will listen to the ways that students help us consider this principle in ever more concrete dimensions. We need to keep reminding ourselves that it was the students we interviewed that renewed our vocation, our response to the call for justice through our pedagogy and our interactions with students, and so now we begin to look at how their words relate directly to the Church's teaching on human dignity. When we consider what it means to respect the dignity of the human person in a classroom setting, a number of themes emerge from the students' perspectives:

- Caring is an essential ingredient of effective Catholic education: not just caring in a broad, whole school sense, but caring that is experienced on a clear and individual basis and that is closely connected to respect for the worth of the individual.

- High expectations for each individual student, not just for the group, give students a sense of their worth as persons and as learners.

- The content and strategies we use in the classroom communicate our respect for the dignity of the individual and the dignity of learning, honoring each student's heritage and life experiences.

It's all about caring

Jessica and Andy, two enthusiastic seventh graders, articulated the importance of caring in the classroom when they said:

Jessica: *Knowing that someone cares about you changes a lot the way you feel. Someone, their mother might not care about them, so what's the point to do anything? But then when somebody do care about you, it makes you change your actions. It makes you change the way you think things and do them.*

Andy: *If you know your teachers actually care, you'll try your hardest in there so you like make them feel proud of you and have them feel real good about you. But if you know the teachers don't really care, or they seem like they don't care, why would you care? That's what it makes me feel like.*

Like Tameka, whom we cited at the beginning of this chapter, these students challenged us to see how a climate of caring is a fundamental requirement for Catholic schools committed to respecting the life and dignity of the human person. We tried to uncover what the students actually meant by caring and we asked each group to describe a teacher who had really shown that he or she cared. Students were eager to answer that question and we began to see what a caring environment actually looks like from their perspective. The students' emphasis on caring or its absence confirmed much of what current educational research tells us: namely that caring is a pre-requisite for establishing an environment for children that is conducive to learning and achievement (See *"Resources for Further Reflection,"* for resources on caring).

Students defined caring in the student-teacher relationship in a variety of ways. As Jasmine noted: *"I think all teachers care. All teachers want to see students succeed. It is just their approach."* For the students, it may be a matter of common sense that all teachers care, otherwise why would they choose to become teachers? On the other hand, some might argue that this student is being overly generous in her assessment of her teachers. We have all worked with colleagues whom we would not characterize as caring individuals, having become jaded or burned out. For the majority of teachers who do genuinely care for the students, there is truth in what Jasmine tells us: we can approach our caring in different ways.

The students we spoke with often described a sense of caring that goes beyond mere sentiment and good feelings, to a more active stance on the part of the teacher for their individual students and the group. In the educational literature, these different "approaches" have been characterized by Nel Noddings in two ways: caring in the *virtue* sense and in the *relational* sense (Noddings, 2005). We think it is worth taking a moment to examine Nodding's work briefly since caring was such an essential part of the message we heard from the students about good teaching. According to Noddings, caring in the virtue sense defines teachers who say they care for their students. They are diligent in investing great amounts of time and effort at being good teachers, and they do care, but sometimes they are unable to create feelings of care and trust with their students. These teachers have predetermined goals for their students (i.e., passing the state test; getting homework in on time, etc.) and *"often work hard at coercing students* (i.e., 'homework free day,' detention) *to achieve those goals"* (2005, p.1). Caring for these students is equated with good teaching and coercion, and sometimes even punishment. The students recognize their teachers as caring, but do not in fact feel cared for. When we look at caring from the relational perspective, however, we look beyond the claims of the teachers to see whether the students think that the teacher is caring. Noddings found that teachers who are at this relational level do not have predetermined goals for their students, but are motivated by the needs and wants of their students. This is not meant to suggest that the teacher's judgment and experience is absent in this relationship, for as Noddings writes:

> *This does not mean that I will always approve of what the other [in our case, students] wants, nor does it mean that I will never try to lead him or her to a better set of values, but I must take into account the feelings and desires that are actually there and respond as positively as my values and capacities allow. (2005, p. 2-3)*

As you listen to the voices of the students, you will hear about both types of teachers: those operating from a virtuous sense and those from a relational sense. When you listen closely, you will see that the teachers identified as more relational are those having the greatest impact on the learning and school experiences of their students. It seems that these are the teachers who are able to establish the relationships of respect and trust that the students spoke about so passionately.

Observe

As I look at my interactions with my students, do I seem to use virtuous caring or relational caring in my classroom? How do I know this? Would my students see me in a different way?

Students stressed the importance of *caring for them as individuals*, echoing the Church's emphasis on the dignity of every individual person. Two eighth-graders provided this insight during one conversation:

Tim: *... a lot of kids have more problems than other kids. They [the teachers] just need to maybe sit down just show that they care. . . . if you want to be a good teacher, show that you care. Just help your students.*

Tiffany: *I tell them don't judge a student before you get to know them. In other words, 'Don't judge a book by its cover . . . don't judge a student by who they are before you get to know them.*

These students have linked two essential elements of our work in the classroom: 1.) students in the same class have very different characteristics and challenges; and, 2.) we must guard against making quick judgments that color all of our work with individual students. In effect, they are urging us to establish a classroom in which we will always take the time to reflect on the changing needs of our students and ways in which we can respond to those needs. They suggest that if we want to maintain a climate of care in our classrooms, we have to implement the call to respect the dignity of the individual person in more substantive ways.

In a similar way, a group of seventh-graders told us that students know if a teacher gives up on them or when they have been marginalized in the classroom:

Christian: *You should never give up on a student because if you give up on a student and they feel like okay, no one cares about my learning so I guess I'll stop. And then that's why students are dropping out of high school now because most teachers are giving up on them and you should never give up.*

David: *You know they give up on you when they stop helping you and stop giving you advice.*

Michael: *When a teacher could be helping you – then he'll just walk away. That's probably when a teacher's giving up on you. If you don't understand and if you're trying to understand it, he or she will just walk away.*

David: *The teachers who are dedicated, stick with us and they won't just give up or push us into a corner and we won't never learn it. Ms. J. she don't ever give up. She will work her bones to get you to pass.*

John: *The best teacher I ever had in my life was Mr. Peter Smith. Man, he was a good teacher. He was a great teacher. We was in a group at St. Mary's and he just made us feel like his kids. I mean he still do. He loved us and we loved him. He took us to a higher level. He took us places, took us fishing and to the amusement park. We always thank him.*

We also heard how some students experience actual confusion when a teacher gives up. For example, Deondre told us: "*Well, my reaction is that if a teacher doesn't care because I failed one of my classes then I don't know what to do.*" It is clear that students are more aware than even we ourselves may be about the frustration and even hopelessness we may convey to a student who is not learning or behaving as we hope.

Another way we learned about how students experience care was by hearing them mention teachers who *reach out to them beyond their class work,* seeing them as individuals. We went to those teachers and interviewed them about how they create a caring environment that enhances the dignity of each person. At one school, many students mentioned Ms. Murphy, a sixth-grade teacher. One student said: "*Ms. Murphy, when we're having a problem she can tell . . . she'll talk to us about it.*" Ms Murphy later described her approach:

You will hear a lot of children say Ms. M. does a lot of preaching but she always tells you right. And when they come in, in the morning, I don't know what happened in the home before they got to me. So when they get in there I try to look through, look at their faces, look at their demeanor, their body language. And if I see one sitting there, I'll say something really funny, something like, 'Who beat you with the ugly stick this morning?' Something like that to just break it away from them and ask what's wrong. That's caring. What's bothering you? Is there anything I can do for you? And then it helps to kind of let them know if they want to talk they can. If you can, you do it away from the others. I try to remove it because children have a tendency to carry it and they harbor it, but if you work with them, you can remove it from them just by talking with them and letting them talk to you.

Ms. Murphy personalizes the climate of care in her classroom, going beyond the parameters of her lessons, and the result is students who perform better because they are confident of her concern for their lives outside of school. It is interesting that she referred to "preaching," an approach that we all know can turn students off, and yet in her case it works. We speculated that the difference may be that her "sermons" spring from genuine caring for the individual not from a desire to control behavior by the force of her will or her statements. Students are astute in their ability to distinguish between care and control, between support and authoritarianism. These young students, in fact, confirm the distinction Nel Noddings made between virtuous and relational caring.

Observe

It is interesting to reflect on the ways in which you let your students know that you care about their lives outside of school. Is there a link between caring and behavior in your classroom? How do you students respond when you "preach" to them?

Students also emphasized the importance of being able to *trust* a teacher. A teacher in one school was particularly well regarded by the boys and trust was one of his defining characteristics. As Charles told us:

Mr. Smith, the thing about him — he was a real person. He never ever told us a lie. He never told us anything that would steer us in the wrong way. He never told us anything that was going to hurt us . . . he never let us fail. Mr. Smith wanted us to succeed.

A number of students told us about teachers who respect their privacy, like John, who said: *"The reason I think Mr. Johnson is a good teacher is because he keeps it between you and him, not the office . . ."* Teachers develop trust by knowing their students well. As Maria noted: *"He knows everything about me and knows how to help me in my work and knows what I going through and don't tell my business either."*

We also interviewed teachers whom students said they trusted. Ms. Lyons, a seventh-grade English teacher, said:

> *When I deal with students it has to be genuine, because they have to feel that it's very genuine. They'll say easily, 'Oh, that teacher's a put on. She doesn't really mean this or that.' It has to be genuine and it has to be a sense of caring. You have to nurture them in such a way that they know you care.*

This same teacher reflected on some of the behavior problems in her school. She speculated that some of the problems were related to teachers who do not have a climate of care in their classrooms. In her words:

> *I can say that there are some teachers who don't care. I can sense that they don't care and the kids sense it, too. They never say that to a kid but the kids pick up on it and when the kids say it to me I don't respond — but they're right on the money.*

As we analyzed more closely the interviews and looked at the classrooms we observed in the school, we realized that many behavior problems seemed to be more common in classrooms where students believed the teacher did not care for them.

The students gave us examples of teachers who seemed uncaring to them. When they described these teachers, they told us that a *lack of caring leads to behavior and learning issues:*

Shanice: *When a teacher shows that she cares, I start to care about her because . . . when I learn that they care about me, I start to show them more respect and listen more to them because when you think somebody don't care about you, you don't pay no attention to them and you don't care about them.*

Theo: *Like, I know one teacher. She kept comparing us to other people. You keep comparing us to other people, we won't learn nothing unless YOU learn something new. That's why we act the way we act. And she compares us to different types of people. Like today she compared us to Chinese people – how they know how to speak our language better than we do. And comparing us to other classes – we're not like them classes. We're all different people. We think different. Stop comparing us to other classes. It's harder for some kids.*

We also see that such lack of care can have a negative impact on the quality of learning for children. As one young man said: *"I think I would have done better in class if I would have known they cared about me. I don't know, it seemed like they didn't care at all. They were just there to do their job."* It seems to be genuinely stressful for students to be in a classroom where the teacher does not convey a caring attitude. Jason told us: *"If you going through some things at home, there's a lot of stress. Then you come to school, and then you get more stress on you."*

Observe ✧

We shared the quote about "Chinese people" with teachers in the school where students had said it, and during the discussion of the students' words, one teacher said: *"That was me that the student was talking about. I never looked at it that way. I thought I was motivating my students."* Can you think of a time when your attempt to motivate your students may have compromised their dignity as persons? What in your actions or words may have done that?

Many sixth-graders at one school talked about Mr. Boyd, a science teacher who was particularly caring. In our interview with him, Mr. Boyd described another aspect of respecting the dignity of the student when he talked about his *role as the adult in the classroom*:

27

Here they can be a kid. I'm the grown up. I got it covered and that's what I would tell them. I got it covered. I got it under control. You can worry about what you need to learn here and what you need to do and I want to make it very pleasant, bright, secure for them. I remind them, though, that I do understand when you go back to wherever you live, where you come from, your home (which is a wonderful place I'm sure) – I understand that you need to become who you need to become again. So I want to say for a lot of kids that's a relief for them. You don't have to come in, you don't have to worry about fighting – and I don't mean fighting each other, I mean fighting for yourself, fighting for your space. Like I said, I have it covered and you come in here and be a kid and let's have fun learning.

Mr. Boyd clearly understands the basic need for safety and emotional security that each individual has. He is demonstrating a depth of understanding of the requirement to respect the particular needs of children, needs that are different in some ways than our own needs as adults. He also demonstrates his understanding of child development and its importance in the classroom. The students also described some of Mr. Boyd's personal characteristics. *He knows how to crack a joke and he won't yell at us if something happens.* One student summed it up when he said:

I think about Mr. Boyd. Like, he's a role model to all of us because he's so fair. There's no words to explain him. He's just always there. He's someone that you can, if you're mad at something, you can go and talk to him and he'll just tell you flat out what you need to do, what you don't need to do. He'll cut through whatever else and just get to the point. He'll tell you.

Observe

You might take a few moments to reflect on the ways in which you create a classroom climate that assures students that "you got it covered." In what ways do you support the students as children in order to free them to learn?

Students returned frequently to the ways in which *respect* is related to caring, making it clear that they see the two as opposite sides of the same coin. One group in particular told us in the clearest terms about respect for the human person:

Jane: *When a teacher cares about me it causes me to respect that teacher more and behave more as I should with them because they take their time to help me and I should take my time to help and respect them.*

Donte: *Yes. Because if somebody respects you, you should respect them back, because you should do unto others how you want to be done unto.*

Joseph: *When they give us respect, we give them respect. We got equal trades. They do their work. We do our work. We do everything for them and they do everything for us. That's all it about, it's respect, that's all.*

Donte: *It would help us if the teachers show us respect like they want to get respect. I mean we're probably not adults, but we want respect just like they want respect.*

Students repeatedly noted teachers who make them feel respected. One of those teachers engaged with us in the following dialogue about respect:

Ms. Peters: *Well I think we grown ups and kids are not defining that word in the same way. I think when kids are talking about respect they mean respect my feelings, respect what is important to me, make that important to you, validate my priority list. I think adults are often talking about behavior: do what I say when I ask you to do it, do it in a timely fashion. I think oftentimes the word gets bandied about but I don't think we're talking about the same things because again I think kids are talking about a much more interpersonal thing and I think adults are talking about really just come in, sit down, be quiet, get the book out, have a pencil, have a piece of paper.*

Interviewer: *That's very interesting but what could we do to bridge that?*

Ms. Peters: *I think to talk more about what the kids actually mean by respect. So I have to spend time going, 'Okay, this is why we're not going to do this' and I'm more than willing to say what is appropriate for the streets is one thing but what's appropriate for institutionalized life is really different. It's changing the paradigm that they're used to working under and trying to explain why I want it this way, why this is going to benefit you in the long run and I find that it's very effective, much more effective than assigning detentions, I've never seen a detention do anything.*

Interviewer: *How does this affect the teacher-student relationship?*

Ms. Peters: *The first thing that came to mind in thinking about the student teacher relationship was respect, mutual respect. I think it is number one. I make them understand that you respect me and I will always respect you. It does not mean I will not get in your face, it does not mean I will not tell you like it is, but I will respect you in all of that . . . there are boundaries, we have to respect each other's boundaries. I tell them right away what my triggers are. They know and that's only fair and so I have them write on a little card to tell me something about yourself and because they've already heard me say what my triggers are, they tend to tell me what theirs are and so I go through those cards.*

From listening to Ms. Peters we can understand why the students identified her as a caring teacher and gain insight into what makes them feel that teachers care about them, know them well, and respect them. Her interpretations of the students' perspectives, highlighting the conflicting definitions of respect, are particularly important for teachers to consider in light of the Church's call to respect the dignity of the person. She reminds us that this call goes much deeper than the behavioral aspects of respect that we often consider. She provides practical ideas for how she creates a climate of deeper respect and care in her classroom.

Observe ✐
Think about the dilemma that Ms. Peters highlights. Do I define respect in
a different way from my students? How do I show them respect? How do
they show me respect? Do we talk honestly about what respect means to
all of us?

As you may remember, Tameka told us earlier that students cannot get a
good education unless: *"the students they care about themselves."* She, like
many of the students, understood the shared responsibilities inherent in
the teaching and learning process. In an interesting way, they recognized
how important it is for students to respect themselves enough to take
responsibility for their own learning. As one student noted: *"You can't
blame it all on the teachers not teaching. It's part of our fault, too . . . in order
for them to teach, we have to pay attention."* Another student put it this way:

> *Most people say they don't get a good education but the reason is
> because they ain't paying attention or they don't do their work. But if
> you pay attention and do your work and follow the steps, you be getting
> a good education. Some people blame it on the school system or blame
> it on the teachers when it is really them not paying attention. You don't
> come to school to have fun. You come to school to do your work.*

We were surprised initially by the students' expression of shared responsibility for their learning. Often as teachers we assume that students resist
responsibility and need to be taught to be responsible. However, what we
heard suggests that many students already understand their responsibility
but may not always have been motivated to act on it in meaningful ways.

Students were readily able to talk about their own personal efforts to be
successful learners. For example, we heard from Joshua that: *"If you want to
learn you're going to learn . . .if you want to learn algebra you go learn algebra. I mean if you're determined to learn algebra nothing's going to stop you."*

In a slightly different way, Peter articulated this commitment to learning when he shared his belief that:

> *God don't make mistakes. Whatever happens, happens, you know. I mean if I fail, I'm not going to let myself fail. That's out! But whatever obstacles be put up I'm up for the challenges because I like challenges, too. Like I said, God don't make mistakes. But failure is not failure. Failure is just something that is a steppingstone — something that you need to step up on and tighten up on. I don't believe in failure and I don't believe in weaknesses just because God don't make mistakes.*

Joshua and Peter both seem to urge teachers to find ways to nurture motivation. Often we use extrinsic motivation techniques because we are not even aware that students like Peter and Joshua have untapped reservoirs of intrinsic motivation. If we respect the dignity of each student, we will look for ways to help them develop the self-respect that leads to confidence and determination to succeed.

Observe

: What are some techniques you use to encourage intrinsic motivation in your students? Can you think of conversations you have had with students about their motivation to succeed? To what extent do your students respect themselves as learners?

High Expectations

One of the best ways that teachers can support the dignity of each student is by holding high expectations for their academic and personal growth. When we talk about high expectations, often we refer to raising standards, raising test scores and improving behavior. Such a perspective is limited at best. It ignores important expectations such as intellectual curiosity, intrinsic motivation, divergent thinking, love of learning, risk-taking, and an ability to work with others. High expectations demand that we recognize and address the best in each of our students in all of their diversity. If we hold high expectations for every student as well as ourselves, we ensure that the goals we set are achievable and realistic.

The education literature is full of evidence that supports the need for teachers to hold high expectations for their students at all grade levels, if they are to be successful in school (see *"Resources for Further Reflection"* for references on this topic). And nearly every school in its mission statement refers in some way to assisting students to meet their full potential. As teachers, we sometimes think that we are the only ones in the school who are expecting a lot from the students. Our stereotypes of children may tell us that unless we are pushing them, many will try to get by with as little as possible. Yet once again we were surprised that, without prompting, the students with whom we spoke often expressed their eagerness for teachers to hold them to high standards and to challenge them to perform and succeed. In almost every group we interviewed, students made mention of teachers who: *"push us to do our work," "who expect a lot of me,"* and *"who never let us give up."* Even some of the weak students or "troublemakers" we interviewed brought up their desire for high expectations. Jason, a sixth-grader, told us:

> *My teacher who really cares is Mr. Jasper. When you come in his room you can learn. He don't mess around. He talks about learning. He approaches us like we be able, by talking to us about our work. That's one of my best classes, because when I come in there I am ready. I know I be learning something for the day.*

Two eighth-graders in another school said:

Thomas: *They help us learn what we need to know and they give us extra work that we're going to need in high school and get us prepared for it.*

Anna: *I feel so proud to be here. Like the math is ninth grade math we're doing. Some people might not understand it, but we're getting there. We're taking it step by step.*

When we consider the students' comments in light of Catholic social teaching and the call of the Gospel, we can see the connection between the educational research that urges high expectations and the essential need to value the dignity of the individual person. If we truly value each person, we can do nothing less than expect that each student can meet the highest academic and personal standards. While students clearly have a sense of the importance of high expectations, it is our job as Catholic educators to ensure that they fully understand and respect their own potential. As Sam told us: *"Our teachers tell us that we're going to make it, and they don't just tell you, 'Oh, no, you're not going to be anything."*

Mr. Ford, one of the student-designated effective teachers we interviewed said:

> *I show a great deal of respect in them as individuals and as people and I think they take that and they return the favor so to speak. Plus I have a great deal of respect for the subject matter I teach. I'm very serious about what I teach and I come across as an authority in my subject which I'm still not an authority here but I kind of play that game and they take me very seriously.*

When Mr. Ford lets the students know how serious their work is, he communicates his confidence in them as scholars. He reminds them that they are involved in hard, important work and that message elevates their own sense of the value of their education. In an interesting way, Mr. Ford is also illustrating another of the social justice themes of the Catholic Bishops, the dignity of work (USCCB, 1998). By respecting them as scholars, he affirms the value of their work as learners, further respecting their dignity as human persons.

Often we as teachers seem to think that many, if not most, students are looking for the easiest path they can take, particularly in the upper elementary and middle grades, but the students told us a different story. Several voiced the same opinion as Justine who said: *"Sometimes I don't think I'm being challenged enough . . . so I'm not able to renew my skills and what I already know."* Her classmates responded:

Nick: *That's right because some of our classes are just way too easy for us. I feel I'm not challenged because the math is everything we learned last year and I'm not being challenged because this stuff is all easy.*

Shanika: *I think it was yesterday. It was an algebra problem and it was so hard, but I liked that brain teaser – that's what I'm calling it. A math problem that you had to write out — and it wasn't just a regular math problem. It was a long, long math problem. That's the kind of thing we need to challenge our grades a bit. I mean make us understand more. If we just sit here and do this easy work like they're giving us, like the work we did last year, we don't need that. We need a fair break. That's what we want.*

Nick: *We in seventh-grade and they giving us multiplication. And they always talking about "You in seventh grade. You need to start acting like you all in seventh grade." Well, teach us like we in seventh grade!*

Some teachers are vexed when students say such things. We can hear them saying: *"If the work is so easy, why aren't the students doing better?"* or, *"But they don't know their multiplication facts – how can I move forward?"* We may need to think more about whether our methods of assessing students create opportunities for them to demonstrate their understanding of the content being taught or perhaps we need to look for alternative methods of instruction. The mismatch in students' and teachers' perceptions of the challenge in our classrooms is worth exploring more deeply. For example, teachers can look for ways to help students assess their own learning more effectively and teachers and students can work together to plan strategies that challenge students appropriately. Ultimately such actions serve to enhance the dignity of the student and the work the student does.

Another student provided additional insight into this dilemma when she advised teachers to: *"Worry more about their education than their discipline."* It may be that the challenge students seek is related to their eagerness to be treated more as capable learners than as behavior problems. Catholic educators have always prided themselves, rightly so, on the effective discipline that supports the education in our schools. Students, however, are suggesting that we must also pay very close attention to the nature of our expectations for their academic performance, that compliant behavior is not enough if we are truly respecting the potential and dignity of each student. We must also respond to the research that shows that discipline problems often occur when curriculum and methods are not fully engaging. If we hear what students are saying, we must continually ask ourselves if we are expecting enough from them academically, not only in terms of outcomes on tests, but in terms of challenging their intellect in effective ways.

Observe ✍

You might want to reflect on how "education" and "discipline" are related in your classroom. Is discipline the precursor to learning or does good discipline flow from students who are challenged and engaged in learning?

Just as the students we interviewed seek high expectations in their academic work, they also want high expectations for their personal actions. Bill said:

36

"You have to be kind of hard on them or they won't do what they're supposed to be doing." We asked what he meant by being hard on them and he added: *"Like stay on their cases, like call their parents when they need to be called."* His friend added:

> *Like Mr. Lester, he always stays on our tail and he never let us slack up because say we're slacking up in class, he'll get on us and call our house, or he'll give us like a little tap on the head like, 'Come on, you gotta do better.' He gives us like speeches and he tells us stories from his life. He makes us confident because he teaches us what we need to know and how we need to act.*

Another student also told us that teachers can be strict while at the same time respectful when they care and show high expectations. Joshua shared this recollection of one of his elementary teachers with us:

> *He was a real strict person. He was out of the army but he had a gentle heart . . . He cared for everyone that came in his class. If you did wrong you had to deal with him so that was like my favorite class.*

When we asked him what happened when you had to deal with the teacher, Joshua proudly replied: *"I wouldn't know. I ain't ever been in trouble with him, but I heard it was gruesome though."*

Even younger students thrive when their teachers communicate their high hopes for the future. Vince beamed when he said: *"It just makes me feel good when the teacher boosts you up and tell you you can be somebody. It makes you feel good."* Vince reminds us of the earlier reference from the Catholic Catechism that states emphatically that justice demands that the person be treated not as something, but as "someone."

We became aware that in the students' perceptions, certain teachers affirmed the potential of individual students more effectively than others. A number of students talked about Mr. Gibson, a thirty-plus year teaching veteran. They told us that they would not let him down because he expected so much from them. We interviewed Mr. Gibson about his expectations for his students and he talked about his approach in his all-male math classes:

> *There's just too many short term fixes so I constantly keep trying to think what's the big picture — and the big picture is help them mature because the problem is that they're immature — so help them mature. With my boys we do a lot of talking about manhood: How do you define manhood? Has there been a man in your life that you've ever seen that you feel like you could model? Often the answer is no so I'll say, 'Think of the adults in your life — how do you like them? Is this a version of adulthood you're shooting for? Do you not like it and if you don't, what do you need to do differently?' Why are you here? Why are you in school? Why is this even important? Why does anybody care? Because I find many of my kids don't have that framework. Here they have to go to school and do well. Okay, but why and wherefore? Especially when they're coming oftentimes from homes where people haven't gone to school, haven't done well so they don't even have an experience of that in their world. You have to know them.*

Clearly Mr. Gibson sees his role well beyond teaching math to eighth-graders. Many students referred to these conversations they had with him and what they learned from these talks was that Mr. Gibson expected them to become good men as well as well-educated men. Repeatedly, they told us that he made them think that it was possible for them to achieve high personal and academic goals and because of that they did better in his classes. Mr. Gibson's relationship with his students reinforces the notion promoted by Catholic social teaching that we: *"can satisfy the need for interpersonal dialogue, so vital for human existence, finding there the reflection of God himself, the definitive goal and fulfillment of every person"* (*Compendium of the Social Doctrine of the Church,* 2005, #133). Mr. Gibson provides a great model for communicating high expectations to our students.

Effective Teaching and Learning

When we started to listen to the voices of students, it was not long before we saw the clear connection between the Church's concept of the dignity of the human person and the practices we use in our classrooms. When we listened closely to the students' words about their classroom experiences, we realized that if we are to respect the dignity of each child we teach, we must also respect the dignity of their work in our classrooms (respect for the dignity of work is another of the themes of social justice). The students made a clear link between these two concepts when we asked them to describe the actions of a caring teacher. A large number of them answered this question by describing caring teachers as the ones who provide them with high quality learning experiences. Tracey said: *"Teachers who care, help you learn stuff. You learn new things and you learn good things, too."* Devonne added: *"They help you understand. Like if somebody doesn't understand something then they sit down and teach you and help you understand what the problem is. They just help you."*

Students want us to maintain our focus on their learning. For example, two students complained:

Kristin: *One teacher she talk about who you dating and stuff like that. I want to be really learning stuff and we don't do nothing in there. I think when I go in there I'd rather read, take out the paper and read and stuff like that, but she just want to talk about what you all are doing, what teachers you don't like, who's going to beat up who.*

Duane: *We come in ready to learn, but when we be in there all we know we're going to do is talk, and she's going to talk to us about city stuff, who we like and stuff like that. And we want to learn an education.*

39

After listening to conversations like these, we soon realized that our teaching practices are directly related to our Gospel commitments to serve the students in our schools. The way in which we most effectively demonstrate our respect for the life and dignity of the human person is to do the best job we can of teaching the students in our care. When we truly respect them as God's children, we can offer them nothing less than the best practices that are available to us in the classroom. Fortunately, the students have given us some important clues as to what will work in order to achieve that goal. In our interviews, we asked students to describe the classroom practices that help them learn the most. Their responses were almost like a textbook on best practice in a graduate course in education, once again affirming the educational research that promotes the use of learner-centered, developmentally and culturally-responsive pedagogy (See *"Resources for Further Reflection,"* for more information on these topics). All of their comments confirmed the importance of a meaningful curriculum and of teaching strategies that engage students in ways that enhance their learning.

Observe

This might be a good time to consider the strategies you already use in your classroom that seem to help your students learn the most. What content seems to capture their interest? What teaching strategies get them fully engaged in their learning?

A number of students emphasized the content of the curriculum and the need for teachers to demonstrate the relevance of what they are teaching. One particularly engaging student said:

> *Another thing that makes us learn is because it's something that we want to do. Like when we said about civil rights. Because when you go back through history books, you see. You know how you watch a movie, and you don't understand why they did stuff like that and you want to go to the teacher and ask them, 'Why did they hassle*

people like that?' You want to learn about it; that's what you want to learn. Say you want to be a civil rights leader when you grow up or be in Congress or something like that. You want to know what's politics and you want to know what deals with that. You want to learn what it is about.

Two other students described curriculum that is meaningful for them in this exchange:

Jason: *A teacher who helps me learn is my social studies teacher. She helps us learn about geography and all about the world and stuff. Like when you grow up and you want to go places, you already know where you're going and what map to take and what country or city you're going to.*

Stephanie: *She also give us a project on religions to teach us about the religions, like if you go to certain places, you'll know the religions and stuff like that.*

The students who are describing these classes are reminding us that content that is meaningful and engaging provides the "hook" that encourages and challenges students to learn by making clear the relevance of the learning.

Several students in one school said they learned the most in Ms. Taylor's class. When we interviewed her, one of the first things she said was: *"They trust you if you're teaching them something they need to know."* She acknowledged that it is not always easy to establish the relevance of everything we teach. There are some things that students simply need to learn, but she understands that relevance is an essential dimension of her teaching and she is committed to being straight with her students about the ways in which they learn. She expanded on this approach when she shared with us:

We have a lot of little talks at the beginning of the year. One of the talks is I'm not going to teach you anything that really doesn't mean anything to you in life. There are some things that I have to teach you because they say that I have to teach you and I make sure they understand why they learn those things. Some kids think they just come here and we just teach them anything. We talk very quickly about "Did you know that there are some things we have to teach? There are places that tell us what to teach." And I give them a copy of my syllabus to understand what they should expect to learn and to show them there is a plan. And I say, "Remember those things I told you I would tell you. This is a really important thing for life, for you to know.

Ms. Taylor believes that teachers improve the learning environment when they actively work to point out the relevance of knowledge and skills. She respects her students' need to think about the reasons for learning, reasons that can motivate them to be more involved in acquiring knowledge and skills. At the same time, Ms. Taylor does not just talk about relevance, but seeks concrete ways in her lesson planning to make connections to the things that her students know and have experienced. Ms. Taylor provides us a good example of how we respect the dignity of our students when we engage them as partners in their learning by discussing what drives the curriculum and our teaching.

Noah is an example of the type of student who benefits from teachers like Ms. Taylor. In talking about what works for him, Noah commented that:

I would remember more when a teacher would connect it to something that we already learned before or that we would use or something that happened. Like they would tell us a story that used it so then we could remember it and make it fun. Like I was never good at taking notes because I would just write it all down and forget to look at it later, but just like remembering it and laughing about the funny stories he told like stuck with me.

Similarly, Susan described how one of her teachers, Mr. Brown, helped her learn: *"He like gives us examples and tells us stories about what he's saying that relates to the subject. And he asks us to put our input and our knowledge in it, too."* When we questioned Mr. Brown about his approach in the classroom he explained:

> *I feel like I give them the background information and just context for them to hang their own learning on. It doesn't matter how I want them to get it. They're going to get it the way that they get it. I think that's what really makes all of us the individuals that we are. I think a lot about multiple intelligences in the classroom setting because each one of these kids really has their own strengths as far as how they do things and how they perceive things so I think that by setting up these projects I give them a way to learn. Because I have kids that are into music, so they bring in music that's relevant to the culture work. And I have artists and I have organizers. They're running around 'you do this and you do that.' I think that it's very, very important that they understand that I am here for a reason and that they are here for a reason and that it's symbiotic. And as far as problems or things that they need help with — that's also why I'm here — that I'm here as a teacher.*

Mr. Brown sees his role extending well beyond guiding students through the textbook or developing lesson plans. Students often complained about only doing worksheets, reading out of textbooks or copying overheads. Mr. Brown recognizes that the students need a context for their learning, that in planning his lessons, he must include ways in which students can hook new learning to prior knowledge or experiences. In order to do that, Mr. Brown also needs to know his students well. One of his students actually said: *"You want to know about things. You want to know about yourself."* Mr. Brown confirmed this when he shared with us:

> *I just take time to learn about them and what they're like. What I give to one I can't give to another. I have to learn those children and that's a big part of teaching, learning what you have in your room. You have to get to know your students. I think that's the key. You have to develop a relationship with your students if you want them to succeed.*

Mr. Brown knows that only by respecting the life experiences of the individual learner and using his knowledge of the students in his lesson planning will his class succeed academically and meet his high expectations for them.

Observe ✐

You might reflect on the ways that you make learning in your classroom relevant for your students. What connections do you make to the students' own life experiences? How do you connect lessons to their family heritage or to community experiences? Can you think of times when you have or could have discussed with your students how what they are learning is relevant to them now or in the future?

At the beginning of this chapter, we heard Pope John XXIII emphasize the importance of allowing human persons to exercise their God-given intellect and free will. In educational terms this translates into choice: choice of what to read, choice of how to demonstrate understanding, and choice of whom to work with. When students are given choices, they begin to exercise more ownership and engagement in their learning. Two students explained this requirement for justice:

Elena: *. . . in this school, they don't give us choices on what we will learn. Like when Ms. Martin taught the book, nobody wanted to read it. So she said, 'Take out your books and read,' and everybody's like 'No' because they don't want to read it.*

Mary: *If we was able to choose something that we like, maybe we'd be more interested in the book and want to read it. . . . They just like give us stuff and so that's what we got to do. I think the teachers should give us an opportunity to choose what we want to do. Like if we wanted to do something in science, they should let us write down all our opinions and look over them and see what we wanted to do.*

As we did, you may cringe as a classroom teacher when you hear this. Our own reaction is to say: *"Well, school isn't about what you want to do; it's about what you need to do."* But when we considered students' comments in relation to the call to respect their personhood through exercise of free will, we began to think about the ways in which we might be able to provide more opportunities for choice in our classrooms. We do have the freedom to be creative and to work with students to make choices that will make their learning more meaningful to them. We can provide multiple texts that they might choose from in Literature Circles, a choice of assessment modes that reflect their multiple intelligences, or choices in the learning strategies that students will use to master material.

Another aspect of effective learning that students emphasized was teaching for understanding. When we asked them what it meant to get a good education, many said that understanding is a key to quality learning. Several students gave us insight into their need to understand:

Maria: *Put a little bit like you care. . . . let me explain these directions' or 'Let me help you out.' We need directions. . . . you need to break it down in lay terms. You can't just give us a paper, and expect us to do it. That's not how it is.*

Chris: *Yeah, like Ms. Suarez, she try to pound everything in at once. But Mr. Neal, he go step by step.*

Jeffrey: *Like we was supposed to get up and read our paper and try to persuade her [the teacher] but she didn't teach us how to persuade. She just read out the book and we had to write five paragraphs. But I didn't know how to persuade nobody using that voice.*

The students are actually pointing out some essential principles of good classroom practice. As teachers we have learned the importance of "scaffolding" learning, of building a structure (scaffold) for learning that will take a student from where he or she is, step-by-step to a higher level of learning. That is precisely Chris's concern. Maria and Jeffrey made us think about the times that we have been disappointed in students' performance on an assignment and failed to recognize that they had no idea how to do what we were asking of them. Until we listened to the students with attention, we did not really focus on the relationship between respecting their dignity as learners and making sure that we are providing structures that support their learning.

Observe

What choices do you provide in your classroom academically and socially? Can you think of examples of how you scaffold learning for your students?

Students also tell us that their understanding is enhanced when teachers make connections across the disciplines in the content of their learning. In the following exchange, students are describing interdisciplinary instruction:

Gina: *Our teacher blends our science with math, reading, social studies, every other subject. So they could help us on every single subject and not just science. Our math and science teachers work with each other. The math and science classes do a whole bunch of things together.*

Shawna: *Like we talk about space **and** we talk about evolution and everything. And that's what we learn in social studies. So in science you kind of know that and it help us out more in social studies.*

Gina: *It helps us to understand anything they're teaching by giving us a new way to think about it.*

Another conversation between students serves to describe the effects on learning when teachers integrate the disciplines:

Rich: *We was learning about social injustice in English. Then when we go to social studies we was learning the same. Basically, all of the classes are related to each other.*

Interviewer: *When the classes are related like that does that help your learning?*

James: *Yeah 'cause some people might not get it in social studies but pick it up in English.*

Carmen: *It gives you like a different view. Like you can see things in different aspects. You can see one way in English and a different way in social studies.*

In our own classrooms, we sometimes have forgotten that in order to develop our students as genuine scholars, we need to help them recognize the ways in which different aspects of learning build upon each other. Mr. Brown noted: *"I would say to me it goes back to one of my favorite sayings that 'the whole is more than the sum of its parts.'"* If we want our children to do more than learn isolated bits of information, if we want them to be able to achieve higher levels of cognition, we need to help them learn to use their intellect to make meaningful connections within and across subject areas. As grade level and cross grade level teams work together, they can identify ways to reinforce the interdisciplinary nature of knowledge and the ways that students can apply skills across the curriculum.

Observe

In my classroom, do I emphasize learning facts and skills or making connections? How do I help my students focus on the "big picture"? In what ways do I integrate learning across disciplines?

As you have seen up to this point, we found that students were providing us with insights into some of the most sophisticated aspects of teaching and learning – but we must admit that we had to interpret their words in order to see those ideas. They could not have been clearer, however, when we asked them about the specific teaching strategies that help them to learn. Just listen to this conversation:

Damien: *I don't like just the teacher puts something on the board and is telling you what it is. I like doing hands on projects and having the teacher come around and talk to us and see what we're doing and like have something that's fun but still helping us learn.*

Sam: *I learn a lot in science because we do a lot of hands on material with chemicals. Right now we're building cars with friction and axles.*

Damien: *It helps us like if a car would break down we would know how to fix it. And then after we're done we say, 'Thank you, Ms. Powell, for teaching us that, because if we didn't, I wouldn't have learned it.'*

Sam: *When we're doing something we get to see how. We don't just get the book terms, the book definition. We get our own experience and what it really is and we can define it ourselves.*

Josie: *I like doing experiments, 'cause I always believe that when we make learning fun, we learn more. We just sit in the classroom and copy notes from the book and copy things from the board and stuff. I mean, we learning, but where is the fun? It is boring and dull. You want to get engaged. So you got to make learning fun. That's why people fail, if you ask me, cause they don't have an interest in it.*

In our teacher training and professional development, we have learned about the importance of active learning, but no education textbook ever made it clearer than these students did. When students are actively involved, they learn better. If our goal is to have them reach the individual human potential we talk about in our mission statements, it would be foolish to ignore what they are telling us. And yet, too often because of the pressure to teach so much to our children, we forget that it is counter-productive to be concerned more with the breadth of our teaching than with the depth we provide in our lessons. Perhaps Josie got it right when she equated fun with engagement.

Many of the students we interviewed complained somewhat bitterly about the quality of the actual lessons they experience in school. Listen to these students as they describe the strategies their teachers use:

Tameka: *I can get more focused on having fun and learning, instead of learning and just being boring and the teacher just sitting up there giving us a lecture or the teacher giving us a worksheet. Have some fun like games and stuff.*

Donte: *But usually we just read a book, then do worksheets. Read the next thing, Then do a worksheet. That's not teaching.*

Maria: *It gets played out. It gets boring doing it over and over and over again.*

Tameka: *Don't talk so much. Don't have a dull voice like blah, blah, blah, then blah, blah, blah. It's boring.*

Donte: *When the teacher gets really excited about what she is teaching then it makes us want to learn. Be excited. Be interactive with us. Put yourself in my shoes.*

It seems to us that these students are asking us to be passionate about our subject matter and enthusiastic in our manner. They want to know that we care about it enough for them to care about it.

Interestingly, we also had students comment on their observations of their teachers' level of preparation, which they saw as both helpful and at times detrimental to their learning. Take for example this exchange between Michelle and Lisa:

Michelle: *To me what makes it harder to learn is like when teachers are not organized and they just be scratching their brow looking for their plans and stuff and they just take time away from the classroom.*

Lisa: *My teacher had all his stuff planned so there was no stopping him for nothing. He knew everything he wanted to do. He told us what we were going to do before class even started.*

It can be hard for us to hear comments like these. None of us is trying to make our lessons boring, and we sometimes resent it that students seem to want to be entertained all the time. But when we examine their comments more deeply, we begin to see that what they are asking for is simply good pedagogical practices that respect them as learners, practices that respond to what we know about the learning process.

The students actually provided examples of the kinds of strategies that they find particularly effective. Many teachers already are doing these in their classrooms. Consider these strategies described by a variety of students from different schools:

- Mr. H. helped us a lot because he did writing workshops. We had read the book *Where the Red Fern Grows* and we had to make movies in different groups. He taped the movie and we had it real good because he helped us a lot.

- And field trips. In that class, we learned about the Jason Project and then we went on a field trip downtown and it was real neat and that got us more interested in science.

- I notice that when Mr. L. tells a story, everybody be quiet and stuff and they listen. You don't hear no talking like when you got paper work all day.

- My math teacher last year played math games and stuff, too. He helped us the same way, and we got math better because the way he explained it, and gave us more ways. He gave us all kinds of ways we could do it.

- We need to do more hands on things. At the beginning of the year we were learning a lot in science. We did hands on things but then we just stopped doing that and we started taking notes, and we didn't learn nothing from that because we need to do more hands on things.

- Our social studies teacher like acted it out so we can really visualize it and he like gives us examples and tells us stories about what he's saying that relates to the subject. And he asks us to put our input and our knowledge in, too.

- I'd like to say math class because we're doing this project with the restaurant and it's teaching us how to take orders. And when you know how to write it down and just add up the math and stuff. Because you have to do with math your whole entire life. Without math, you aren't going to be able to get a job or stuff because you have to figure out the profits very fast.

- I learn in that class because we get to be able to have like, discussions about things.

We can see that all of the strategies that students have described involve active learning. We asked students what advice they would give their teachers and Thomas told us: *"I'd tell them to try and be creative."* Their ideas caused us to think about what we know about child development in relation to the Church's call to respect the dignity of the person. Through childhood and early adolescence, students are concrete thinkers who learn best when they can use their senses and their experiences to build their learning. If we use that information consistently in planning their education, we may be doing the best thing we can to respect the "growth process" that the Church urges us to affirm.

How do we judge our response to the call to respect the dignity of the human person?

By listening to the voices of children throughout this chapter, we have heard them calling us to justice in our teaching practice and our interactions with our students. We have been privileged to learn more about ourselves, about our teaching, and how our work relates to the Catholic Church's call to practice justice by respecting the life and dignity of each person. We have found it to be one of the most profound validations of the work that teachers do to hear the students' thoughtful input on caring teachers, high expectations, and effective teaching practices. Whether we see it every day or not, students are paying attention to their schooling and they are making judgments about how they learn best. They, too, are observing and judging! Their perspectives give us an outstanding opportunity to evaluate our work in new ways and to make decisions about our own classroom practice as well as the attitudes and approaches that we will expect in our schools.

When we use our students' voices to guide our work, we must consider their individual human dignity. Indeed, we as Catholic educators have a special obligation to ground our teaching practice in that very principle for: *". . . when we look into the eyes of the human person, we see there the greatest manifestation of the grandeur of God, the clearest reflection of the presence of God among us"* (Kreitemeyer, 2000, p. 22).

A number of years ago, we conducted a writing workshop with an eighth-grade class. At the end of the semester, they came to our university to share their personal writing with undergraduates who were studying to be teachers. Near the end of a very moving afternoon, we asked the eighth-graders to give the pre-service teachers advice on how to be good teachers. Immediately Janita's hand went up. She had been one of the most difficult students in the group, refusing to write on many occasions and often negative in her interactions with us and with her peers. Reluctantly, we called on her and she said: *"If you want to be a good teacher, look us in our eyes so that you know what we are thinking and feeling."*

The most venerable document on Catholic social teaching could not say it better. Janita has laid down the most fundamental principle that teachers could follow: to fully respect the individuality of each person by looking deeply into their hearts and minds. We can do no less if we are to be true to the call of the Church and the call of our students to respect the life and dignity of the human person.

Discussion

Throughout this chapter we have taken time to observe aspects of our own teaching practice and of the expressions of justice in our schools. Following Pope John XXIII's urging, we now can take time to judge the ways in which we are effective in our response to the Church and our students and the ways that we can respond more fully to their call. Teachers might begin by sharing some of their observations they have made throughout this chapter about respect for the dignity of the individual in their classrooms and in the school as a whole. It is certainly important to begin with the positive things we already do. Another step may be to talk about any surprises we heard from the Church and from the students quoted in this chapter. You may also decide to use some of the following questions as a starting point to tackle the more difficult task of sharing candidly the ways in which you can deepen your shared commitment to justice in your school and make sure that you regularly examine how your actions can fully respect the dignity of every student.

Possible Questions:

1. Sharing our observations (be as specific as possible):

   - In my classroom, how do I live or make evident the fundamental dignity of the human person? In what ways would my students describe me as a caring teacher?

   - How does my classroom practice let each student know that I value and care for him or her as an individual?

   - How do the teaching strategies I use demonstrate my respect for the dignity of the individual and the dignity of work in my classroom?

   - How might my students interpret my attitudes about their value as individuals?

2. Judging our whole school's respect for the dignity of the human person:
   - Discuss the same questions above, but consider the school as a whole during your discussion

3. As I (we) listened to the Church and the students in this chapter, what did they say that surprised me?

4. Deepening our shared commitments:
   - Are there ways that I/we may communicate a lack of respect for the dignity of individual students?
   - Do I/we communicate realistic, high expectations for all students? Do some students get the message that we do not expect them to succeed? What leads them to hear that message?
   - Does my/our teaching practices adequately address the needs of all students? If not, what may be the barriers to success for some students?
   - Are there ways in which we fall short of creating a true climate of care and respect in our school?
   - Do I/we spend more personal/professional energy on discipline and classroom management than on academic excellence?

CHAPTER THREE

They Call Us to Community

" In a global culture driven by excessive individualism, our tradition proclaims that the person is not only sacred but also social. . . .the Catholic tradition teaches that human beings grow and achieve fulfillment in community."

—*USCCB, 1998, p. 4–5*

When we asked students at one school to describe a teacher who cared about them, we had fascinating discussions with several groups of students about an unusual class meeting that changed the quality of the student-teacher relationship and the teaching and learning environment for both the teacher and the students. Variations of the story went something like this:

Danielle: *One of our teachers, she used to be real mean. She took one day to sit down and talk to us and now she's nicer. She looked to our point of view and actually asked us, like how do we think she teaches.*

Tanya: *We were shocked that she would actually ask our input on how to teach.*

Danielle: *We changed a lot. We started acting better and listening to what she had to say and she started listening to what we had to say. And she gave us more time to think.*

After we heard the story a number of times, we began to ask additional follow up questions and we learned more about what happened with this teacher. According to the children, things were very difficult in her classes. The teacher told us she could not get this group of students to behave and, more importantly, she knew she was not teaching them what she had hoped since she was spending all of her time trying to control their behavior. She AND her students were angry and frustrated. The students told us that the teacher had brought in another teacher to help them work the problem out with her. In effect, she tried the technique of mediation, which we so often use with students, to address her relationship with the students in her classroom. They were shocked that their teacher actually let them tell her what they did not like about the climate and the learning in the classroom. And we were shocked that this teacher had achieved a complete turnaround with this class, for now the students were describing this as one of the most caring and effective classes in their school.

As we thought more deeply about what we heard, we realized that these students recognized another essential aspect of caring and the importance of community as another basic element of social justice in schools. They had experienced caring from a teacher who was approaching her students as a community who could help her grow as a teacher. These young students had, in their own way, affirmed that:

> ... the dignity of the human person makes sense only in the context of person's relationships to others in the community. Human dignity can only be realized and protected in the context of relationships with society (Kreitemeyer, 2000, p.23)

This educator and her students alerted us to new ways for schools to create communities of relationships where students and teachers can grow and develop together.

As you read and discussed the previous chapter, you saw that the students provided great insights into the reality of Catholic social teaching in our schools. When we asked them about their education, we had no idea that they would tell us things that related directly to the most basic principle of Catholic social teaching, the life and dignity of the human person. Once we examined their ideas through the lens of the Church's teaching on justice, we saw that much more of what they said related directly to the principles that are at the heart of the Gospel call to justice and embedded in the Bishops' themes of social teaching, particularly those related to community, to the rights and responsibilities of individuals in a community, and to solidarity among all persons. As we delved more deeply into their statements, we could not miss the connection between what they told us about the dignity of the individual and what they had to say about the communities that we create in our schools.

What does the Church mean by community?

" How we organize our society . . . directly affects human dignity and the capacity of individuals to grow in community . . . . Our Church teaches that the role of . . . institutions is to protect human life and human dignity and promote the common good."

—(USCCB, 1998, p. 4-5)

Just as Genesis tells us that we are made in God's image, it also affirms that human persons are created to live in community. In the account of creation, one of God's first statements after the creation of Adam was: *"It is not good for the man to be alone; I will make him a helper, suitable for him"* (Genesis 2:18). The account goes on to say that God then created animals to help Adam in many ways, but it was not until God created woman that Adam declared: *"This is now bone of my bones and flesh of my flesh* (Genesis 2: 23). Pope John XXIIII described the essence of this relationship when he wrote that the human person is essentially a social being because God, who created humanity, willed it so (*Pacem in Terris,* 1963). Catholic social teaching stresses that human persons are capable of communion and cooperation with each other in society. *The Catechism of the Catholic Church* defines society as:

> *. . . a group of persons bound together organically by a principle of unity that goes beyond each one of them. As an assembly that is at once visible and spiritual, a society endures through time: it gathers up the past and prepares for the future (2000, 1880).*

This might be an equally good definition of "society" in our Catholic school classrooms. We are bound together with our students in the way that Tameka described in Chapter Two: *"You need students that care and teachers that care. The teachers they care about the students and the students they care about themselves."* Students and teachers, already grounded in the centrality of the individual person, move on to establish relational bonds that are "visible and spiritual." Students recognize and respond to these relation-ships in their actions in the classroom. We also use the past wisdom and teaching of the Church in order to prepare our students for the future. The Church is emphatic in stating that: *"Social life is not exterior to [persons]: [they] can only grow . . . in relation to others."* (*Libertatis Conscientia*, #567).

> **Observe** ❧
>
> Reflect on the ways in which your classroom is a small society as the catechism describes society. How are students "bound together" or unified in your classroom? How is care for each other visible in your class-room? What spiritual connections do you see?

The common good, an essential element of Catholic social teaching, is another of the concepts that we seem to assume we understand because it is so much a part of our earliest ideas about our faith, as well as our notions about American democracy. But the Church has defined the common good in specific ways that bear on our role as Catholic educators. *The Catechism* (2000) states: *"By common good is to be understood the sum total of social conditions which allow people, either as groups or as individuals, to reach their fulfillment more fully and more easily"* (#1906). Once again, the Church reminds us that the mission statements of our schools, calling for each person to reach his or her full potential, place requirements of justice on us as Catholic educators. *The Catechism* demands that we look analyti-cally at the: *". . . sum total of social conditions. . . "* in our classrooms in order to achieve this universal goal of Catholic education. *The Catechism* goes on to explain that the common good is made up of three essential elements: 1) *"the common good presupposes respect for the person as such"* (#1907); 2) *"the common good requires the social well-being and development of the group itself"* (#1908); and 3) *"the common good requires peace, that is, the stability and security of a just order"* (#1909). We shall see that each of these elements has a direct relationship to life in our schools.

One of the most important concepts to emerge from the Church's teaching on the common good is the way in which the value of each individual leads to the greater capacity of the group. *The Catechism* actually states that we must seek to attain: "*. . . objectives that exceed individual capacities*" by valuing the varied contributions that individuals make to the group. St. Paul described the importance of valuing the ways in which individuals contribute to the good of the whole when he wrote:

> *Now to each one the manifestation of the Spirit is given for the common good. To one there is given through the Spirit the message of wisdom, to another the message of knowledge by means of the same Spirit, to another faith by the same Spirit, to another gifts of healing by that one Spirit, to another miraculous powers, to another prophecy, to another distinguishing between spirits, to another speaking in different kinds of tongues, and to still another the interpretation of tongues. All these are the work of one and the same Spirit, and he gives them to each one, just as he determines. (1 Corinthians 2.7-10)*

Paying attention to the contributions of individual students is essential to promoting the common good in our schools. Pope John XXIII noted the relationship between the individual and the group when he stated very clearly that no one is exempt from cooperating, according to each one's possibilities in developing the common good (*Mater et Magistra*, 1961).

The Church's teaching also relates these ideas about the common good to the central place of the family in human life. The teachings regarding family have implications for the "second family" that we create for children in our schools where children spend so much of their time during their formative years. In a letter to families, Pope John Paul II affirmed this when he defined family as: "*. . . a community of human life, as a community of persons united in love*" (*Gratissimam Sane*, 1994, #874). If we look on our classrooms as an extension of the child's own family, John Paul's further point is even more important: Every child: "*becomes a gift to the entire family, who cannot help but feel its presence, its sharing in their life and its contribution to* *their common good and to that of the community of the family"* (*Gratissimam Sane*, #884). Reflecting on these words, it is imperative that we create a sense of family in our classrooms.

The Church expressly values the primary role of the family as educators, *"uniquely suited to teach and transmit cultural, ethical, social, spiritual and religious values, essential for the development and well-being of its own members and of society"* (*Charter of the Rights of the Family*, 1983, p. 9). As Catholic educators, we take on a sacred responsibility when we agree to support families in their work of educating their children in all of the ways outlined above. Teachers frequently talk about the ways in which families make our work in the classroom more difficult. The Church's teaching suggests that we must look beyond these impressions and think creatively about how we can enhance the partnership we have with families.

Closely related to notions of community and family is the Church's teaching on solidarity. The call to solidarity: *"proclaims that we are our brothers' and sisters' keepers"* (USCCB, 1998, p. 5). In the Bishops' description of solidarity, they look at the importance of justice in a global sense. When we looked at this theme, it seemed only natural for us to see that the school and the classroom is "our world" in educating our children. We wondered what the notion of solidarity looks like in the world of our schools. John Paul II instructs us that community requires: *"a firm and persevering determination to commit oneself to the common good; that is to say to the good of all and of each individual, because we are all really responsible for all"* (*Sollicitudo Rei Socialis*, 1987, #38). Throughout the Gospels, Jesus calls us to the "new" commandment to *"love one another, even as I have loved you, that you also love one another"* (*John* 13:34). This commandment of mutual love is at the heart of the Church's teaching and it is also essential to our work as Catholic educators. Jesus demonstrated his complete solidarity with us in His death on the Cross. His example teaches us that: *"life in society, despite all its contradictions and ambiguities, can be rediscovered as a place of life and hope . . . an invitation to ever more involved forms of sharing"* (*Compendium of Catholic Social Teaching*, 2005, #196). The Church's teaching on solidarity speaks to our vocation as teachers who are committed to the common good and the good of the individual students served. It further requires that service be an essential response to the commandment to love one another. It certainly affirms our work in Catholic school classrooms to remember that we have the opportunity to help children fulfill the promise of Christ's death and resurrection as they develop their solidarity with others.

Observe

These ideas may be difficult to connect to our work with young children, but try to reflect on how your classroom brings to life the notion of solidarity. Can you think of examples of times when students seem to truly stand with you or each other in their life in the classroom? How do they seem aware of responding to the good of one's neighbor?

In chapter two, we looked at how the child's work in the classroom contributes to his or her dignity as a human person. The Church also asks us to see a relationship between individual work and building community. John Paul II urged us to see that each person's work is connected to the work of others. He wrote that, today: *"more than ever, work is work with others and for others. It is a matter of doing something for someone else"*(*Centesimus Annus,* 1991, #832). The first work of our children is the work they do through their participation in school. That effort makes them: *"heirs of the work of generations and at the same time shapers of the future of all who will live after us"* (*Compendium of the Social Doctrine of the Church,* 2004, #275). As teachers we tend to see learning happening within each child, but the Church's teaching and the students we interviewed stress the communal nature of their development, for the individual's: *"productive effort cannot yield its fruits unless a truly social and organic body exists"* (*Quadragesimo Anno,* 1931, #200). Children will learn better in classrooms that are true communities of learners.

What do students tell us about community?

Just as respect for the dignity of the individual person is a requirement of Catholic social teaching, we cannot be effective as Catholic educators unless we develop a strong sense of community in each classroom and in the school as a whole. The students we interviewed helped us envision community in new ways by sharing their perspectives. They provided insight into the practical ways in which we can enhance the communal nature of our classrooms. When we consider the call to community, a number of themes emerge from the students' perspectives:

- Care and respect are not only experienced on an individual basis, but must be the foundation for developing a sense of community for the classroom and the whole school.

- A true school community is built on a notion of family that respects all the relationships in the school: students and teachers in the classroom, collegial relationships, and home-school connections.

- A strong sense of personal responsibility and service is essential in order to develop a caring community.

Certainly every Catholic school strives to create a Christian community, but these students described a view of community that gave us a clearer picture of how we go about doing that. The question for us became: how can we as Catholic educators re-vision our notion of community in our schools and create a community of learners that supports individual students and teachers and promotes the common good most effectively?

It's (still) all about caring

You may be asking yourself: *"Wait a minute – didn't I already read this section?"* Yes, this was the title of a reflection in the previous chapter! But it seems to be the only title that works here. If we want to respect the life and dignity of the person, it is all about caring. And if we want to create community – it is all about caring! The concepts presented in the seven themes of Catholic social teaching are very difficult, in fact impossible, to separate. As we analyzed the students' words, however, we came to believe that the subtle differences that relate to the various themes of Catholic social teaching are worth exploring. By visiting – and revisiting – the students' insights we begin to build a clearer picture of how we as Catholic educators can be shaped by Catholic social teaching and how our Catholic schools can become even stronger when teachers are fully grounded in this teaching. Just as the students helped us to identify caring as the foundation for respecting the individual, they helped us to see that a climate of care is an essential ingredient in creating a community of learners. To begin to sort out these subtle differences, we return to the story at the beginning of this chapter.

The students described a classroom that was seriously lacking in community at the beginning of the school year. The students did not trust Ms. Overton and by their own admission, the classroom was chaotic. When Ms. Overton tried to find out what was wrong, her students would not even tell her the truth. Anita told us: *"She asked us what we think of her and we did-n't tell her what we really thought. We just said she was okay. But you're just a little mean and you don't teach as good as the other teachers."* Ms. Overton was not satisfied with the outcome, so she asked a fellow teacher to facilitate a more substantive discussion with her students. This is how one group described the process:

Anita: *We all sat down and she gave us a chance to talk about what we thought was going on. Ms. Overton she put inputs on it and said what she thought was going on. We said, "Like you're one of those teachers who think they have to be strict in order for the kids to learn really well. But then when the other teacher came in, we found different words and we changed it. Instead of saying she was real mean and stuff, we said she was 'a little aggressive' maybe. And we had to like change the words a little so it would be respectful.*

It is worth stopping here to note that we do not see this kind of interaction often in schools. As teachers, many of us are reluctant to let students know that we are stumped about what to do in a particular situation. Opening ourselves up like this in front of our students is risky, as it puts our vulnerability on the line for all to see. Like so many classes, this one had been taken over by negative forces that might have seemed to need a tough response. When that did not work, Ms. Overton took a chance on a process that invited her students to take more ownership for a climate of caring, and the outcome was very positive. The students described it this way:

Anita: *We came up with a solution to try to make the classroom a better working environment.*

James: *That we would just start over and act like the first day of school and act like we don't know each other and give everybody a fresh start and forget what happened in the past.*

Danielle: *She used to explain it one day and we didn't understand and then the next day give us a test. But now we do projects and we're doing a current group project right now on Africa and we all have a region of Africa and we have to do an oral report on it.*

Observe

Can you think of a time when you or a fellow teacher involved the students in decision-making about a problem in the class? Did that problem ever involve your own interactions with the students? How did that change the sense of community in the classroom?

This story was part of what led us to see that students actually are calling us to see our role as Catholic educators in ways related to Catholic social teaching. All we had done was ask the students to describe a caring teacher, but they told us how community had become reality in their classrooms. Their sense of community was enhanced because their teacher took a risk. From their point of view, she demonstrated in a powerful way that she wanted a caring and respectful community in her classroom where each individual contributes to the good of the whole. Throughout the student interviews, we built new insights into what factors contribute to community in schools.

One of the first factors that contributes to community, so well demonstrated by this teacher, is the importance of teachers actively modeling respectful interpersonal tools for building community. The interpersonal techniques that we use are one of the ways we demonstrate the level of care we have for each other. She genuinely wanted her students to learn and she knew that the relationships in the classroom were a barrier to their academic achievement. When we interviewed her, she said:

At first the girls really wanted to rule the classroom. I had about six girls who were very strong. They had strong leadership qualities and unfortunately they were competing with me for the control of the classroom. They were very, very angry.

This teacher cared enough about her students and their learning to bring in a colleague to "mediate" the problem that she and her class faced together. She communicated to her students that resources and techniques are available to solve community problems. Together the two teachers demonstrated strategies for analyzing a situation. They proposed solutions and agreed on outcomes. For example, with the teachers' help, the students practiced the kind of language that contributes to understanding. Remember when Anita told us that the students: *"changed the words a little so it would be respectful."* Her teacher described it this way:

We agreed on consequences and I told them that if they showed me the respect that I deserved I would give them the respect they deserved. I said you come and tell me there's a problem I'll work around it, but just the fact of saying that made a tremendous difference. It wasn't a totally smooth ride from there on out, but I think that they came to realize that there was a point of mutual respect and they knew when they crossed the line. It doesn't become whether they like me or not, it becomes understanding that they are in here for a purpose and I'm here to move that along.

The students in this class came away much better equipped to confront difficulties not only in school, but perhaps as well in other social settings. Together they had taken steps to create a community of care.

Similarly, Ms. Jeffries, another teacher we interviewed in the same school, emphasized the importance of opportunities to involve an entire class in solving community problems among themselves. Like so many of us, she worried that students used talking about class problems to avoid schoolwork. She overcame this concern by looking at these situations as opportunities to build community and to teach. Ms. Jeffries told us:

> *I tell the students 'I need to get through this lesson. I know this other problem is important to you. Can you hold onto this for one day and tomorrow I promise we will focus on this but I really need to get through this lesson.' They'll respond to that and they'll go 'Okay, okay, that seems fair, we can live with that, okay.' We can get to it tomorrow – we will give this to you today. But I think that approach to children for some adults feels inappropriate, feels like you're babying – but you're really giving them control, some control over the dynamic in the classroom and very often I think teachers don't feel comfortable with that. They don't feel comfortable letting the kids sort of set up peace.*

This teacher, like the one mentioned above, highlighted another important community building tool – listening carefully to students. It is at the very heart of what we are doing in these reflections. Justin, a sixth-grader, noticed that some teachers are not really listening and told us:

> *You know when someone's not relating to you. They answer what doesn't really relate to what you said and it's obvious that they wasn't paying attention and they just gave an answer: 'Oh, really!'" And you can tell they wasn't paying attention.*

One teacher, Mr. Preston, was very aware of the impact listening skills have on learning. He emphasized that the teacher must model active listening. He noted:

I try to be an active listener and I've learned that in teaching you have to be an active listener. Teaching isn't all telling and I let children tell me. When I'm doing a lesson, I let them discover and learn by telling me. I ask them all the time 'What do you think? I would like to know what you think about that.

Observe ✍

Can you think of a time when community has broken down in your classroom? How do you demonstrate (or could demonstrate) community building tools to your students in order to address their concerns? How do you demonstrate and model active listening?

We are Family

In this chapter we are focusing on the school as a community of learners in which both students and teachers work together to create an environment in which they can grow and develop; a place where each individual's dignity is respected and protected. In listening to the students, it became clear that the metaphor of family was one way of conceptualizing this community. It also reflects the Church's emphasis on family throughout its teachings. For example, the U.S. Bishops instruct us that: *"Catholic social teaching more than anything else insists that we are one family; it calls us to overcome barriers of race, religion, ethnicity, gender, economic status, and nationality. We are all one in Christ Jesus* (cf. Gal. 3:28) - *beyond our differences and boundaries"* (*Communities of Salt and Light*, 1993, p. 10). And as the Church often states, the family is the central or core institution in any community and the prime educator of its children. The parents' right and duty to educate their children is:

> *essential, since it is connected with the transmission of human life; it is original   and primary with regard to the educational role of others, on account of the uniqueness of the loving relationship between parents and children. (Familiaris Consortio, 1982, 126).*

It stands to reason that if the family is viewed as the central social institution in society, and if the family is seen as the primary educator of its children, then the school should, to the extent possible, emulate the types of relationships that define the 'ideal' family. The students and teachers we talked with used the notion of family to describe another component of schools and classrooms where both students and teachers experience a caring community. We see in their perspectives a sense of what it means to be family, and another way of thinking about Catholic social teaching as it relates to the school context.

Students and Teachers in Classrooms

The first relationship we think about in schools is the one between teachers and students. When we asked students to think about a teacher who really cared for them, or a teacher in whose class they learned a lot, students often talked about family in one way or another. The following conversation reflects much of what we heard:

Malik: *I think about Mr. Carpenter.... he's a role model to all of us. I know everybody in my class looks up to Mr. Carpenter ... because he's so fair. He's just always there.... if you're mad at something, you can go and talk to him and he'll just tell you flat out what you need to do, what you don't need to do. He'll cut through whatever else and just get to the point.*

Susan: *He has a calm voice. He don't yell at us. Well, if you make him mad enough he'll yell at us but he talks to us like we have sense.*

Malik: *He knows who we are and he knows we're not little kids.*

Susan: *He treats us like his family.... he won't yell at us if something happens.... if we're arguing he'll say for us to work it out. He's like the only teacher that kind of gets them back together. He's like a father for us.*

In another school, students reflected on the idea of family at a deeper level with one student expressing skepticism when teachers told them they were like their own children. Teachers needed to prove their words by their actions:

Katie: *. . . Mr. Maple treats us like we his children. He knows how to keep us in shape when we out of line.*

Jonathan: *He's like a father figure to me by the way he just sits and talks. It's not like we hide anything. We just talk and I feel more comfortable around him than I do a lot of my peers.*

Jeffrey: *That's how it was at the beginning of the school year with Ms. Phelan. She was telling us that from now on we're her babies. We're her boys and we like family to her. At first I was like, 'OK, whatever.' I'm like "She just wants to get us to do all this work and stuff and be mean," but now I know that she does care because she listens to us. She actually sits down and pays attention and actually hears what we're trying to say to her and she helps us a lot.*

As you listen to the students speak passionately about family, you can imagine how important these types of relationships are to them. They are able to reveal to us the characteristics and virtues of a family, a community, that are important to them: things like fairness, trust, honesty, respect, intimacy, watchfulness, and care. They speak with sincerity and genuineness about their deep longing to belong to a caring community and how they look to teachers to make sure this happens. As adults we may sometimes take for granted that the students feel a sense of community or family in school. The children let us know that we need to be much more aware of how we go about creating this family atmosphere and much more explicit in communicating our desire to nurture such a community to the students. We found, as we are sure you have, that students are very astute observers, able to see through our rhetoric and right to our actions. The students we spoke with made it clear that there is a difference between those of us who talk about a family in the classroom and those who in reality create a family with the students (a good example of Nel Noddings' idea of the distinction between virtuous and relational caring discussed in Chapter Two).

Interestingly, when we interviewed the teachers that students identified as their best, and we asked them what makes them effective teachers, a number of them also talked about creating familial relationships with their students. The teachers identified some of the same characteristics and virtues that the students used to define community and a sense of family. We have put some of the teachers' comments in the form of a conversation that helps to illustrate further the importance of creating a sense of family in our school communities:

Mrs. Cole: *I don't know how this happens every year, but they become like my children and we have a sense of family and that is really a part of who we are here so that's how I define that relationship – one that is based on respect but it has a certain type of intimacy with it once you establish the authoritative kind of roles that are involved. It's tricky and doesn't work for everyone.*

Mr. Gray: *I treat my students like I treat my kids at home and a lot of kids have fallen into that, 'Gee, if he treats me like this I'd like to be at your house.*

Ms. French: *I love them. That's what I tell them.*

Interviewer: *How do you communicate this notion of family to your students?*

Mr. Smith: *It's also what happens outside of school. I've ended up at baptisms. I've been at confirmations. I've been at birthday parties. I've been at funerals. They know I'm there and if you give me an invitation because you're singing a solo at church, usually I try to get there to be there to let you know that I care about you as a person. And I think once they sense that you care for them as a person, they'll follow you any place you want to take them.*

You can hear in what these teachers say that they believe deeply in nurturing this type of community in their classrooms, and this stance has produced the intended benefits as heard in the words of their students. Most of us would like to create that type of atmosphere in our classrooms, and the students we interviewed seem to urge us to examine very carefully how effective we actually are in achieving that goal.

> ## Observe ✐
> As you think about your own classroom in light of the students' descriptions of family-like classrooms, what would your own students say about the ways in which you promote a sense of family in your own classes? Imagine what they might say about how life in your classroom makes them feel that they are part of a family of learners?

Another of the family-like relationships that is vital to the health and well-being of the classroom is that among the students themselves. The relationships among students are another issue of social justice since positive relationships can enhance community and negative ones can seriously limit the common good. When we returned to the interviews and looked for students' references to their relationships with each other, we found a few areas where they highlighted the importance of these interactions.

The students identified one important way that teachers prepare them to participate in community life by involving them in group work that encourages caring and respectful group interaction. Students talked about how these strategies enhance their learning:

Thomas: *Just like when we studied the planets and we wrote a book about the stars. We made our own little children's book and it was so cool. We were all in a group and we each had a part. We put it all together and we presented them. It had to have certain questions in the book, but it still had to be a children's book. A fun book.*

Jane: *It was based on information. We put it in a book and read it to little kids. It made us feel good afterwards and it made you feel like, 'I know these answers.'*

Anthony: *It made you feel like, 'I know about the stars.' And then we learned about the solar system and planets and the sun.*

The same group of students went on to emphasize the value of the group interaction:

Anthony: *When we work with our friends, we can actually put our knowledge together.*

Thomas: *When we go into the lab, we do like an experiment and then we figure it out, but we're using other people's knowledge along with ours. We get a better answer.*

Jane: *It teaches me cooperation, like to help work with people better and life – if I get a job I got to work with somebody. That helped me a lot to be able to work in groups better.*

The teacher led these students to build community through effective group work while teaching the curriculum. So often teachers reject group projects because of worries about whether all students will learn the material or whether they can handle group situations responsibly. In this case, it was clear that the teacher had prepared the students adequately and the learning was, in fact, effective. The teacher also saw the importance of extending the social nature of learning beyond her own classroom by giving her students the chance to interact academically with younger children in the school. When these middle school students read their stories, teaching the material to younger students, it not only contributed to their sense of being part of the school community, but also helped them to learn the material more effectively. It is interesting to note that strong community ties such as these enhance student learning.

Observe

Group work has become a regular part of classroom life. How much do I use group work in my classroom? In what ways do I prepare my students to work together effectively? What tools do I give them for managing group work and producing good results?

Another aspect of student relationships surfaced in our interviews when we asked students to talk about obstacles to their learning. Often they told us that other students were distractions in the classroom. Fidgeting, fighting, note passing, talking, and playing around were most often how these interactions were characterized. It seemed to us that the same actions that frustrate teachers on a daily basis are also frustrating the students – and, interestingly, not just the "good students." Some of the students who joined in these conversations were self-reported "troublemakers." There was one particular group of students that was very concerned about these distractions. One in the group, Peter, despairingly told us that: " . . . *they hide your book bags and take all your paper work and stuff, and we ask the teacher to do something about it.*" His comment made us think about our role as teachers in helping our students solve these kinds of problems. Often we think students know how to interact appropriately with each other, when in fact, they lack the social skills required for solving personal problems. If we are truly committed to the Church's and the students' call to community, we have an obligation to think about how to address such issues in a way that helps to solve the problem, but also models the importance of justice in the classroom.

Whatever the age of the students with whom we work, these sometimes complex and ever-changing relationships and the personal dynamics that are involved in them can be a challenge for teachers to negotiate. When these relationships are not nurtured, when we do not explicitly help our students respond to Christ's call to: *"love one another as I have loved you,"* the consequences can undermine our efforts at creating a just and caring community in our school and classroom.

Faculty Relationships

At first we were surprised when students talked about the relationships among their teachers and how these relationships influenced their view of the quality of teaching. After we thought about it, however, it wasn't surprising at all; young people are always looking to the adults in their lives to get information on how to navigate their world. Often we are so focused on

our subjects and our students that we lose sight of how our collegial interactions – and the quality of other relationships in the school – affect teaching and learning. Students' keen observational skills helped us see how
respectful, collaborative relationships between teachers impact the students' experiences in school.

It is important for teachers to model the types of behaviors that reflect
the family-like relationships that are so desired by the students. On another level, these experiences also speak to the solidarity among faculty members that is vital to creating healthy and vibrant communities where both
students and teachers flourish. Solidarity or collegiality among faculty
responds in a way to John Paul II's statement that: *"Yes, human beings are
their brother's and sister's keepers. God entrusts us to one another. Our freedom has a relational dimension; we find our fulfillment through the gift of self
to others"* (*Evangelium Vitae*, 1995, #19).

For those of us in Catholic schools who seek solidarity with each other,
we ourselves grow in relation to each other and we model respectful, caring
relationships for our students. A sense of community and collegiality
among teachers provides models to support student learning and the
opportunity to share their expertise with each other. However, creating
such collegiality is not always an easy task. As teachers, we are often socialized to work in isolation from our colleagues. Collaboration can be challenging due to time constraints, personalities, and individual goals. Sometimes collegiality involves risk-taking and challenging our colleagues,
which is difficult when we are trying to create family. And sometimes there
is even competition among faculty that impedes our working together. A
notion of solidarity, central to Catholic social teaching, challenges us in this
regard. To quote the U.S. Bishops: *"we all belong to one school community. As
such we have mutual obligations to promote the rights and development of
both students and colleagues. We need solidarity for our success and that of
our students."* One of the teachers, Mrs. Finley, said it best:

> *I think the staff has to come together and we all need to try to be as
> close together and on the same page as possible. We need to sit and*

talk about what works for me. That might not work for another teacher but that teacher might be able to take some of the things that might be working for me and try them in her class so that we all can be asking the same thing of the child so the child does not feel I'm here and then I go to this teacher and I'm there. Children are in a state of confusion and they don't really know what you want.

Observe

Thinking now about your relationships with colleagues, how would you describe the level of collegiality between you and other faculty members in your school? What are the factors in your building that encourage and/or hinder efforts at collaboration and collegiality? Can you describe how students benefit (or don't) from the level of collaboration between you and other teachers in your school?

Family-School Relationships

Most teachers understand that good relationships between families and the school are vital to students' success in school, yet they are often the most challenging relationships to cultivate. The U.S. Bishops' Task Force on Catholic Social Teaching and Catholic Education (1998) stated that: *"all institutions have an obligation to respect the family and to foster and protect it, not undermine it"* (p. 24). As Catholic educators, we have a vital role to play in this part of the Church's social mission, and the ways in which we invite families to participate in the education of their children is a key element in promoting justice in our schools.

As we talked with the students, we became aware of the fact that they almost never mentioned a relationship between their own families and the schools. This surprised us since teachers and administrators so often talk about this relationship. The few students who did bring this up in conversations usually spoke of it in positive terms as a way of helping them do better in school. For example, one student mentioned that she knew her teacher cared for her:

... because she would always, like, if I was messing up or something, slacking in her class, she would call my mother and my mother would straighten me out. Or she would have a meeting with my mother to tell her about the difficulties and problems that I'm having and then I would try to straighten up and get my work done. And that's how she helped me.

Another student attributed his success to his teacher talking with his parents: *"She interviewed my parents and that's what helped me get better grades."* In these two examples, a relationship was created between the home and school so that effective communication could be used to benefit the students. This is not always the case, as evidenced by one young woman who had a very different perspective. Amanda's view caught our attention when she complained: *"The teachers are always telling us that what we do here is what we learn at home and my mom don't ever teach me how to be a bad child. She always taught me how to be good so it showed me how to respect people."* Amanda was angry that teachers made inaccurate judgments about her family life without really knowing her family. Her comment suggests one way we might unwittingly undermine the family and their role in their children's education. Further she alerts us to the potential misunderstanding that can arise when teachers make assumptions about their students' families.

Observe

If you asked students in your school to describe the relationship between their teachers and their parents, what do you think they would say? In what ways might different children describe the relationship in different ways?

Nurturing and encouraging parental participation in school may be one of the most challenging tasks of teachers and administrators, particularly in schools where social, economic, and cultural differences exist between the home and the school. Yet we know from research that parental involvement in students' education, however we define such involvement, is an essential factor in student achievement and success in school (See *"Resources for Further Reflection,"* for references on this topic). In light of Catholic social teaching, parents have a right and a duty to participate in their child's education, seeking together with teachers, the well being of their child as well as the good of the school community. In all of our schools parents and grandparents, aunts and uncles, brothers, sisters, and even at times cousins, are active participants in each child's education in a variety of ways. Catholic schools benefit in this regard given our mission and the fact that families choose our schools for religious and academic reasons.

Many of you have worked hard to create very positive relationships with families that are beneficial to you and your students. There are, no doubt, some successful efforts in your schools that promote parent participation. Despite our best efforts, however, there are families who are perceived as un-involved, and these families often dominate our conversations and sap our energies. We have all heard it said in justifying our students' failure that: *"their parents just don't care . . . we don't get any support from the parents."* While there may be times when it appears that this is the case, Catholic social teaching requires that we seek to identify strategies that work to encourage strong home-school connections; that we understand the reasons for a lack of participation; and that we explore ways to address them. Many of the teachers we talked with were aware of the myriad of factors that impact effective home-school connections. Let us look briefly at some of those factors from the perspectives of teachers.

There was an acknowledgement on the part of some of the teachers that parents can feel alienated and unwelcome at their children's school. One teacher said: *"For a lot of our parents, school isn't a comfortable place."* Another commented: *"Sometimes I think parents feel like these doors are closed to them and they can only come in at certain times."* A third teacher added: *"A lot of parents feel alienated. I have parents that say, 'I don't know how to do that math.'"* One story related to this was particularly disconcerting:

> *I've given a kid back a paper that was just horrible. The kid is destroyed because, 'Well, my grandmother helped me." I think well,*

'That was not enough, I'm afraid. Maybe your grandma didn't understand the whole assignment.' I don't want to say she's dumb as a door knob because she may not be but maybe she is or maybe she can't read either.

It is possible that many of the families we work with had negative experiences in school and so there may be a level of distrust or even fear that comes with participating in their child's education. It is possible that we have not always created as welcoming and warm an environment as we imagine. It may be that we do not communicate clearly to parents our expectations and assist them in being involved in appropriate and helpful ways. It may also be that negative stereotypes color our judgments about parents and families. We did talk to teachers who suggested that the challenge of working with parents often resides in not fully understanding the families with whom they work. For example, a novice teacher shared with us that: *"It's so hard for me. I know there are different backgrounds but it's hard for me to grasp the concept of a mother or father not making sure that their student has their homework done."* Similarly another teacher told us: *". . . that I have to take a step back to just reflect on the fact that maybe they live with a grandmother or an aunt. That's not something that I know."* And then there are the economic factors that may make family participation, within the current structure of most schools, next to impossible. One teacher captured this factor when he said:

We have many parents who are working evening jobs. We have many parents who are working two or three jobs and they can't take time off to come to school because they're hourly wage earners and if you miss that day you may not have your job.

One teacher was particularly honest in talking about relationships with families and touched on issues related to trust between the home and school. She suggested that one of the reasons for a lack of parental participation in some classrooms might be the fact that there are: *". . . teachers [who] feel like if a parent's coming in to watch their class, they're out to get you and they want to find out what you're not doing."* We are certain there are many other reasons for poor relations between the home and school. It would be interesting to examine the parents' perspectives on these issues. Whatever the causes, if we are to respond to our commitments to justice and to Catholic social teaching, we need to find ways to foster parental participation so that the families of the children we serve can be brought into our school communities.

Observe

As you reflect on interactions with parents in your own classroom and in your schools, describe the families who seem to participate fully in their child's education. Describe the families that seem disengaged from participation in their child's education? What techniques do you use to encourage parents to feel comfortable and involved in their child's education?

Really Knowing Each Other

Building community in our schools, like nurturing a family, rests in large part on how well we come to know each other. Teachers need to know their students well and understand the communities from which they come. As in any family where each of its members knows the others intimately, the students we interviewed expected that their teachers would know them well. What was less evident, but also important, was the expectation that students would also know their teachers well! One way we respect the dignity of each member of our school community is to take the time to know them. In order for us to promote the common good of all members, we need to know the needs of both individuals and the group. Knowing each other is crucial for creating community and fostering the types of family-like relationships students and teachers hope to establish in their schools. Let's look at how students expressed this notion that teachers knowing their students would have an important impact on their schooling experiences.

One of the most profound expressions of the importance of knowing students was presented in the last chapter with Janita's comment that: *"If you want to be a good teacher, look us in our eyes so that you know what we are thinking and feeling."* We are still taken aback by the impact this comment has on us every time we read it. Janita is challenging her teachers, and challenging us, to come to know our students on a very intimate level – coming to know what students *think* and *feel*. She is promoting a level of knowing far beyond students' likes and dislikes, favorite things, extra-curriculars, and birthdays (not that these are not important as well).

Other students shared similar sentiments. One young man spoke about a teacher who really knew the community in which he lived. In talking about this teacher, Marc told us that: *"she was really into our neighborhood and community things. She was riding past, and she'd see us on our bikes and she'd tell us what's going on. She'll sit down and talk to us about it."* Another student talked about teachers knowing her parents, telling us that: *"She knew our parents and would call our parents. She got to know us, and not just know me as my name."*

Students believed that when their teachers knew them well, this knowledge contributed to their success. Angie, for example, believed strongly that: *"If you're a teacher you should always try to talk to each student individually and find out where they are. Some people catch on quicker than other people."* This exchange about a particular teacher represents much of what we heard:

Ryan: *He knows everything about me and knows how to help me in my work and knows what I going through and don't tell my business either.*

Joan: *He's dedicated to getting to know us better so he can help us. He don't just give us our books and say 'do the work.'*

Ryan: *We would do journal topics and you could write about whatever you wanted. Then he would write back. I liked that because he got to know more about you and you got to know more about him. It was nice because you could ask him things.*

Many middle school students seemed to understand that their teachers needed to be knowledgeable, not only about them as individuals, but also about young adolescents in general in order to be effective in their work. This sentiment was expressed by a number of students. Tameka, for example, suggested that middle school teachers need to: *"Place yourself as the student. Place yourself as you want to be taught. Put yourself in my shoes."*

As teachers we understand how important it is to know our students. The teachers we talked with, identified by their students as most effective, spoke often about this and in a way that mirrors the beliefs of the students. There were those who talked about knowing what their students liked and disliked, what organizations they belonged to, how many siblings they had – the typical type of information that we often gather at the beginning of the year. There were others, like Mr. Pearson, who believed it was important to get to know his students outside of school by attending baptisms, confirmations, funerals, and birthday parties as a way of letting his students: ... *know I'm there ... I try to get there to let you know that I care about you as a person."* However teachers also spoke about knowing their students in terms of their emotional and social background. We think three examples will be helpful to demonstrate the value of knowing our students at this deeper, more complex level. A number of teachers talked about how challenging it is to teach our students when they are experiencing difficulties in their lives beyond school, and that without addressing the various issues our children of all ages face, the teaching and learning process cannot proceed. Mrs. Yates told us what made her an effective teacher:

You have to continually be aware of what's going on in your room and I don't mean who's on the right page, I mean what is socially going on, what's emotionally going on, what's going on at home with your kids. They bring so much before they ever come in here that you have to be aware of that. I think that you just can't sit down and teach them a lesson and expect them to get it if they bring to you problems at home, problems in the classroom. If they are not mentally ready to sit down in your room that day, you have got to do damage control before you can ever teach them a thing. I think that's what people don't understand. It's an awareness. Even if you're working with younger kids, they may not feel good that day, that they may just miss their parents and they're not being a baby, they just miss their parents. I think that a lot of times that's what it is, people are so focused on their lessons, what they're teaching, where the hand outs are, what page in the book that they don't ever gauge where emotionally and socially the kids are and I think that people have to start doing that.

Mrs. Yates recognized the "baggage" students bring to our classrooms, and she respected those issues, and the dignity of each student, by acknowledging and addressing them. She implicitly understands that nothing will be accomplished for the rest of the students if the individual needs of others are not met. Mrs. Yates also raises for us the social dimension of our students' lives. We suspect she was thinking of it in terms of her students' relationships with peers and family.

Other teachers we talked with looked at the social dimension more globally, taking into consideration the cultural and economic factors that impact students' success in school. Here we begin to explore the realm of cultural competence on the part of teachers, something that is particularly challenging when social and cultural differences exist between teachers and their students. Two teachers we interviewed were particularly attuned to this aspect of our students' lives. Mrs. Jensen, discussing her efforts in working with her team of teachers to understand student behavior, emphasized this cultural factor:

They really are authentically behaving in the way that they've been culturally shaped. Most of what they're doing if you really go back into it, really does follow a logical train of thought. It isn't like they've just gone insane. There's a world that they live in where these rules make sense. They just don't make sense in this environment and so that's the disconnect. We have to just keep focused on helping them build a bridge to the difference in this environment as opposed to saying they're wrong and trying to still validate them. You can't just say that's stupid and the way you live is wrong and it's ridiculous because no one's going to respond to that, but you can say that it's appropriate for this situation but it's not appropriate for every situation.

Ms. Yates is describing what the educational research refers to as a cultural 'mismatch' or 'incongruity' between the home and the school cultures that we will address again in the next chapter. Mr. Johnson also alluded to the role that culture plays when he shared with us his struggle with how to talk with his colleagues about why students were behaving in certain inappropriate ways and not achieving at higher levels. He shared his beliefs:

I just think that sometimes it's hard for people who can't think outside of the world where they live and to really try and understand what some of the kids here experience. It goes back to you have to understand what environment these kids come from. Even if they have a two parent home, and some of these families have a better income than my family has so it's not socio-economic, it's just the environment and the culture and the community. It's the Spanish kids, it's the black kids, it's the White kids who come from these environments but often because of the experiences they've had, they have so many defenses about feeling disrespected and so if you're not a person who can understand, really try to understand what that feels like and why that is the way that is, you tend to right away disrespect that child. And you have hurt them. They don't trust you. They don't respect you and it begins to almost become a power struggle and then it's over.

These are powerful statements. They reach to the core of what it means to respect the dignity of an individual within a community, a school community that has been expressly established to: *"provide an atmosphere in which the Gospel message is proclaimed, community in Christ is experienced, service to our sisters and brothers is the norm, and thanksgiving and worship of our God is cultivated"* (USCCB, 1990, p.2). These understandings challenge us to know our students and their communities intimately so that we can use this cultural knowledge to build community and assure the common good.

Observe

You might try to think about interactions in your classroom that show a particular child that you know him or her well. What do you know about your students' lives beyond the classroom? Try to describe a few of your students in as much detail as you can.

Personal Responsibility and Community

Within Catholic social teaching, the U.S. bishops have clearly articulated the importance of the rights and responsibilities of all members of a community to participate fully in that community. In their document, *Sharing Catholic Social Teaching: Challenges and Directions* (1998), the bishops state: *"We believe people have a right and a duty to participate in society, seeking together the common good and well being of all, especially the poor and vulnerable"* (p. 5). This theme has many applications in the school context. In Chapter 2, for example, the students established their understanding of their right and responsibility to participate in school by their desire to be actively engaged in their learning. We have also examined the teachers' responsibility to ensure the dignity of individuals and the common good in schools through their teaching practices and their interactions with students, colleagues, and families. When teachers and students seek to serve the common good, they must share responsibility for building community in the classroom. In this reflection, we will hear the students talk about their desire to participate further by being of service, not only to the school community, but to the larger community as well. We will also examine teachers' commitment and professionalism as one manifestation of their own responsibility.

One of the most encouraging insights we gained from the interviews was the students' desire to take more responsibility for the quality of school life by developing strong reciprocal relationships based on caring within the school community. Jamie, whom you will meet again in the next chapter, was elected president of the student council (which rarely met). He lamented that: *"We don't have a voice or say in anything that goes on here. I try, trust me, I try talking to everybody I possibly can."* They wanted to take more responsibility in much the same way that John Paul II described: *"...a firm and persevering determination to commit oneself to the common good; that is to say to the good of all and of each individual, because we are all really responsible for all"* (as cited in NCCB, 1998, p. 5-6). They told us that students want to be of service within the school: *"Like people should work in the office and stuff. . . .it would be like helping the principal. Teach people about things. Yeah, jobs, at other schools they have jobs."*

A number of young adolescents brought up their eagerness to share responsibility for younger students in the school. You may remember the group of students who spoke so enthusiastically about teaching younger students about the planets. In a number of K-8 buildings, contact with younger children provided the students a sense of responsibility and belonging, two characteristics common among young adolescents and two characteristics important to building community. They saw it as their role to provide an example for the younger children and to be role models. The students also wanted to be of service to the younger children. The following exchange reflects some of what we heard from the students:

Joshua: *We're supposed to set an example for the little kids.*

Tonio: *Like, we should stop cussing. We can show these kids that we can be better than how we are now.*

Joshua: *By setting an example you know. Like if you see them running in the hall, tell them to stop so they don't get in trouble.*

Tina: *We can help out the little kids, you know. Be a role model for them. Like going to their classes, tutor and teach them.*

Joshua: *We should take time to sit down and talk with [younger kids] and see what they need help in or what's the problem. Like if they can't read, ask the teacher, 'Say Mrs. So and So, may I sit down with so and so and help him read because he's having trouble.'*

Teachers and administrators can find so many ways to capitalize on the strong desire students have to be connected to students in other classes and to serve them in a variety of ways. Many of your schools are already engaged in such practices through activities like buddy systems. These practices build community within our schools while at the same time enhancing learning and addressing the developmental needs of various age groups.

In one school students expressed the importance of participating in the larger community as well, as they described a service learning project that connected them to others. One student noted: *"Mr. S wants us to actually get out there and use what we've learned and helping people."* Another boy went even further when he defined a good education by saying: *"He* [the teacher] *encourages us to do good things in the community. He says the most important thing you can learn how to be a good person and that's really cool."*

It became clear to us that students are truly calling us to practice social justice in our actions within the school by urging us to enlist them as partners in making the justice teaching of the Church real in our schools. Not only are they aware of their rights as students, but they are willing and ready to assume appropriate responsibilities for the common good of the school and the community. Their call presents us with an interesting challenge to expand our own thinking about how we teach them to exercise justice within the school and the community, about the opportunities we offer them to act justly themselves.

Our Responsibility as Teachers

Before we move beyond the topic of personal responsibility as it relates to the call to community, we would like to focus briefly on the concept of vocation as it relates to the teachers' commitment to their profession. We see it as our personal responsibility to be the best we can be for the community we serve as teachers. The students we talked to also appeared to understand that this level of commitment is required for teachers in order to be effective. As Jasmine put it so eloquently: *"If that's what they want to do* [teach] *if that's their career, go for it 100%, not just 50% or 80%. Put their very best into it."*

Students surprised us with how acutely aware they are of the difference between teachers who are truly committed to their work, who are called, and those for whom it is a job and a paycheck each month (students' ideas about teachers who are in teaching for the paycheck will be seen clearly in the next chapter). It seemed to us that students understood that a teacher's commitment to his or her vocation is essential to the quality of the community and the quality of the learning experiences required for their success. Students seemed to sense when teachers were not content in their work. In one conversation a student commented: *"When teachers get agitated and it seems like they don't like their job and they take it out on you. What you're really thinking is, 'If you don't like your job, then go get another one.'"*

Interestingly, as students talked about their teachers' commitment to their work, they included a variety of characteristics that defined this commitment. One of those was an expectation that teachers exhibit a level of professionalism which they defined as a teacher's attitude towards his/her work and their demeanor in interactions with others. The students we interviewed had a lot to say on this point, expressing clear expectations about how their teachers should act in the classroom. The students expected their teachers to come into the classroom with confidence. Put simply, one student said: *"They should be confident in what they are doing."* Another student clarified this point when she added: *"They have to come with a strong, positive attitude."* Another student seemed to concur with this, but added a cautionary note: *"You have to show some leadership, but don't push it to the point that they won't listen or they won't respect you."*

The students also talked about a teacher's demeanor. As Jasmine suggested: *"Act mature. Don't be afraid of the audience."* We were intrigued by this statement and asked the student to elaborate further. She went on to explain:

> *Don't act like you do at home. Like if you slouch and stuff, if you're at home, you know how you relax and lay back in the chair? Don't be teaching like that. And if you're sitting down, don't be slouching, sit up in your chair.*

Students stressed the importance of teachers being enthusiastic and having a sense of humor and what an impact this has on their motivation and learning. Byron expected that teachers would *"talk with excitement,"* while Carmen suggested that when teachers are excited: *"It kind of rubs off on you. You might get excited too if the teacher's excited."* A specific example of this came in Michael recalling a teacher:

> *He made social studies real fun. Like I'll never forget one time we was talking about the Civil War and he went in the hallway and put on this hat and these leather pants and went skipping through the classroom. It was just . . . we loved social studies and we loved talking about history. If you don't know about your history you got not future.*

A young man simply put it this way: *"Have a smile on your face when you come into the classroom."*

In their own way, the students illustrated what it means when teachers demonstrate the kind of commitment we heard from Pope John Paul II. To work at fostering and protecting the dignity of individual students while at the same time promoting the good of all in our school communities, we each have to be firmly committed to our call to teach. The Church demands such commitment. The students deserve it. This challenge requires that we reflect on ourselves and our vocation. As one teacher, to whom we had talked, said: *"A teacher needs to look at themselves first. What are you about? What are you really about? When you stand in front of the classroom, what do those children see?"*

The Value of Service

How do we judge our response to the call to community?

In this chapter, we have heard the voices of students as they provided us insights into the importance of community as an essential component of Catholic social teaching. We have to remember once again that we did not ask them questions directly about the importance of community. But when the students reflected on what helps them succeed, they told us over and over again that the quality of interpersonal relationships is what matters most in their schooling. With a consistent voice, they call us to be mindful of the community that we create in our classrooms and in our schools.

Certainly every Catholic school asserts that community is an essential feature of the school environment – after all, we are guided first and foremost by Jesus' call to *"love one another."* Yet the students we have heard remind us that things are not always as we hope them to be and that every school faces challenges to maintaining a family-like community of learners who participate fully in the mission of the school. The best Catholic schools are the ones in which every part of the community regularly takes time to evaluate their efforts to create a fully Christian environment that responds in charity and hope to each other. In these schools, teachers do not just make a global judgment that their school is a caring community. They take the time to look at the subtle signs, the individual interactions, the inevitable missteps that can limit how effectively we ensure a living sense of community for students, teachers, and parents.

Discussion

Just as in Chapter Two, in this chapter we have taken time to observe aspects of our own classroom practices and of the ways in which our students experience community in our classrooms. Once again, following the urging of Pope John XXIII, we now can take time to judge the ways in which we are effective in our response to the Church and our students and the ways that we can respond more fully to their call. Teachers might begin by sharing some of their observations of community in their classroom and in the school as a whole. What are the positive things you already do to promote a sense of community? Then, you might discuss anything that surprised you about the Church's teaching or the students' comments. You may decide to use some of the following questions as a starting point to tackle the more difficult task of sharing candidly the ways in which you can deepen your shared commitment to justice in your school and make sure that you regularly examine how your actions can fully support developing community in every aspect of life in your school.

1. Sharing our observations (be as specific as possible):
   - In my classroom how do I live or make evident a commitment to community? How would students describe our classroom community?
   - How do I encourage students to take responsibility for community in my classroom?
   - What do I know about the families and communities of my students? How do I create connections with the families of my students and with the communities in which they live? How would their parents describe the community in our classroom?
   - How might students describe my relationships with my colleagues?

2. Judging our whole school's commitment to community, family and participation:
   - Discuss the same questions above, but consider the school as a whole during your discussion.

3. As I (we) listened to the Church and the students in this chapter, what did they say that surprised me?

4. Deepening our shared commitments:
   - Are there ways that I/we may limit our effectiveness as a fully Christian community?

   - To what extent do I/we create opportunities for our students to take responsibility for the quality of our school community?

   - What might be barriers to creating community within our faculty?

   - What are barriers to creating community with families?

CHAPTER FOUR

❦

They Call Us to a Preferential Option for the Poor and Vulnerable

" *As followers of Christ, we are challenged to make a fundamental "option for the poor" – to speak for the voiceless, to defend the defenseless, to assess life styles, policies, and social institutions in terms of their impact on the poor.*"

—*USCCB, 1986, p. 16*

IN ONE OF OUR FIRST INTERVIEWS WE MET JAMIE, A VERY IMPRESSIVE, articulate and thoughtful young African-American, eighth-grade student attending an urban, K-8 school. He was a self-reported leader of his class: president of the student council, involved in intramural sports, hard worker, studious. Jamie did not appear to demonstrate the characteristics sometimes associated with urban, male young adolescents. One of his dreams was to attend an all-boys, college preparatory Catholic high school in his city. In response to a question on the quality of the education he received at his current school, he told us a recent story about taking the entrance exam for St. Mary's High School and what he learned about himself and his school experience. He began the story like this:

> *I just took the St. Mary's test a month ago. I took the test and there was a whole bunch of things on it. There were some things on there that we learned and there were some things on that they said I should have already learned ... And I thought I did a good job. But as the test results came back – I know this one friend, he took the test also – and when we compared our test scores, and he goes to Utica [a suburban district nearby]. His test scores were way higher than mine. See I'm not saying I have the highest but I say that I'm in the top three on all my tests [at his school]. I score above average. On this test I had all lows. I thought that personally I did a bad job. I thought I was sleepy or something. I wasn't focused enough.*

Jamie eventually came to see, with the help of a concerned adult, that the difficulty he had on this test was not necessarily due to any inherent weaknesses in himself, but rather, to certain inequities that existed in his schooling experiences that probably accounted for at least some of the differences between his performance and that of his friend.

Talking with Jamie had a profound impact on our thinking. Before this encounter, and despite our mutual interests in issues related to educational equity and justice, we never really thought about students' perceptions or awareness of injustice in their schooling experiences. We knew the impact of injustice on children intellectually, but not how that injustice was being understood and experienced by the students themselves. As we began to explore Catholic social teaching, we saw connections between what the students were telling us and how the Church was speaking about justice. The students called us to think in new ways about some of the issues that impacted their education, and they helped us understand the Church's call to a preferential option for the poor in more realistic and concrete terms. The students called us to define justice more broadly and to reflect more critically about the various inequities, big and small, that exist in our schools and in our classrooms. Here is where we saw the intersection between the Church's call for a preferential option for the poor and Catholic educators' work in schools: acknowledging and addressing the issues and circumstances that privilege some of our students while marginalizing others.

In this chapter we will examine this third bedrock principle of Catholic social teaching. We will discuss the preferential option of the poor as it is defined in the teachings of the Church and embedded in the scriptures. We also will explore young urban adolescents' insights into the inequities that exist in their educational experiences and how their perceptions might further our understanding of and response to the Church's call for a preferential option for the poor in our work as Catholic educators. In many ways, this principle of Catholic social teaching is one of the more challenging. As students uncovered these various inequities for us, and as we began to analyze and think about what the students were saying, we realized that they were posing for us, and for others who might read their words, a significant challenge. They were requiring us to enter a place that many might find uncomfortable, complicated, and difficult. Understanding this, we invite you to examine this principle, along with the challenges posed by the students and the Church, with an open mind and an open heart.

What does the Church mean by a Preferential Option for the Poor & Vulnerable?

" The Church's love for the poor ... is part of her constant tradition. This love is inspired by the Gospel of the Beatitudes, of the poverty of Jesus, and of his concern for the poor. Love for the poor is even one of the motives for the duty of working so as to 'be able to give to those in need.'"

—*Catechism of the Catholic Church, 2000, #2444*

The Church's call to love and serve the poor has been an essential part of her tradition since the very beginning, clearly present throughout the scriptures and in the teachings of the Church. We will define a preferential option for the poor as a commitment by individuals and the community at every level to participate in the struggle to overcome social injustice in an effort to achieve the common good. Put another way, the option for the poor is a way of: "strengthening the whole community by assisting those who are most vulnerable" (U.S. Catholic Bishops, 1986, 16). We want to note early in our discussion that the Church is not promoting an exclusive preference for the poor in its teaching, but rather a response to the needs of all people, especially those with the greatest need. As noted by Peter Henriot, S.J.:

> *"An option for the poor implies involvement in the struggle to transform society with greater justice, more respect for human rights and deeper concern for the environment. We do not take the place of the poor, but we struggle alongside them in the work for social justice." (1997, p. 18)*

But who are the poor and vulnerable and those with the greatest need? We believe that many of the students in our classrooms and in our communities are vulnerable by the very fact they are children. They are the voiceless and defenseless to which the bishops refer. At many levels of our society, the injustices we encounter are often linked to the inequities that exist between the rich and poor, between peoples of different races, cultures, languages, and religions. The roots of injustice are often economic factors which have a devastating and demoralizing impact on the social, political, cultural, and educational experiences of the marginalized and less fortunate. The economic gap, which has been the focus of much of Catholic social teaching from its inception, profoundly contributes to the achievement gap which plagues so many of our students in public and parochial schools. When the U.S. bishops' moral test of: *"how our most vulnerable members are faring"* (a key element of this principle) is applied to the education of many of our nation's students in both public and private schools, the outcomes are dismal.

We think it is safe to say that there are many teachers, certainly among them many Catholic educators, for whom a preferential option for the poor is part of their vocation as a teacher. There are teachers who choose to work in urban and rural schools, providing direct service to the poor whose education is disproportionately impacted by economic, cognitive, physical, social and emotional factors. According to the 2004-2005 data provided by the National Catholic Educational Association, 44.2% of Catholic schools are located in urban and inner-city areas across the country. These statistics point to a significant commitment to direct service to the poor through Catholic education. This is vital work and clearly follows the mandate of scripture and the Church. Teachers who work in these schools often do so because they believe they can make a significant difference in the lives of urban and rural youth. In our interviews with teachers working in an urban Catholic high school, there was almost unanimous agreement among them that the reason they chose to teach at St. Malachi's was due to the school's mission to provide a strong academic background so that students can assume roles of leadership and service. These teachers also spoke of their own personal desire to work with students who have not had the same opportunities as other students.

Many of us, while not providing direct service to the economically poor, are working hard to meet the needs of those who are poor and vulnerable in other ways: students who have special needs, whose learning is impacted by physical, social and cognitive factors; families who struggle with a variety of issues – illness, addiction, unemployment, struggling relationships; those who are bullied and who bully; and students and parents who suffer the pain of racism, sexism, classism, and homophobia. These are the poor to whom Paul VI referred in his encyclical *Octogesima Adveniens* (1971) in which he stated: *"The Church directs her attention to these new poor - the handicapped and the maladjusted, the old, different groups of those on the fringe of society, in order to recognize them, help them, defend their place and dignity in a society"* (#15). More recently, *The Catechism of the Catholic Church* (2000) maintains that love for the poor: *". . . extends not only to material poverty but also to the many forms of cultural and religious poverty"* (#2444).

Some of us are working in schools where most, if not all of our students, are privileged. For those of us who find ourselves in this situation, we would suggest a particular responsibility to reflect on the Church's call to a preferential option for the poor since this principle is such an integral part of the Church and its teachings, and therefore important to our identity as Catholics educators. We further suggest that this responsibility goes beyond reflection to living and modeling love and service for the poor for our students. It extends to guiding them toward an understanding of and commitment to a preferential option for the poor, whether it is through our curricula, discussions, or other school traditions.

The preferential option for the poor is closely linked to the other two bedrock principles we have discussed – human dignity and community. As we have noted, one's dignity as a human person is realized in community. It is in our relations with others that we fully realize our potential and affirm what it means to be created in the "image and likeness of God." Further, a healthy community can only be achieved if all of its members have access to the necessary resources to develop into healthy human persons. Such a community requires that special attention be given to those with special needs – the poor and the vulnerable. As Incandela (2000) states: *"we are not a true community if we leave people behind; and the ones we are most likely to leave behind are those with the least ability to keep up on their own"* (p. 301).

While the term preferential option for the poor is a relatively new addition to Church documents, this bedrock principle has been embedded in most of the Church's social teaching for more than one hundred years and it is rooted directly in the teachings of Christ and the Hebrew prophets. Much of the Old Testament describes the relationship between God and the poor. The psalmist (103:6) tells us that: *"The Lord performs righteous deeds and judgments for all who are oppressed."* The Hebrew Scriptures are filled with references to God's special love, care, protection and defense of the poor. In the New Testament, Jesus continued this tradition of special concern for the poor. He clearly identified with the poor and vulnerable, challenged the rich and powerful, and proclaimed to the poor the Good News. In the *Epistle of St. James,* the writer reminded his readers: *"Listen, dear brothers and sisters. Did not God choose those who are poor in the eyes of the world to be rich in faith and heirs of the kingdom he promised to those who love him?"* (2:5). James was blunt in his question, stating God's call to a *"preferential option for the poor"* in no uncertain terms. It is within this scriptural dimension of our faith that Catholic social teaching is grounded. The writings of the popes and bishops have continued to boldly speak the Scripture's message of a special concern for and identification with the poor in our times. While the term *"preferential option for the poor"* itself does not appear until the writings of John Paul II, the spirit of the concept is present from the very beginnings of the Church's teachings related to its social mission. For example, Leo XIII stated (1891): *"Still when there is a question of protecting the rights of individuals, the poor and the helpless have a claim to special consideration"* (*Rerum Novarum*, #54). More recently the U.S. Bishops' have stated:

> *"As individuals and as a nation, therefore, we are called to make a fundamental 'option for the poor'. The obligation to evaluate social and economic activity from the viewpoint of the poor and the powerless arises from the radical command to love one's neighbor as one's self." (USCCB, 1986, #87)*

This is our faith, our call to justice. The foundations of our commitment to justice for all people, particularly for the poor, are clearly and profoundly articulated in the scriptures and in Church documents. They reflect God's special concern for the marginalized and the oppressed. The message is clear – we are called to: *"hear the cry of the poor"* and respond to their needs so that they are able to participate in community and utilize the resources that are available to all of us for our good and the good of all. For us, this cry is coming from many of the students in our classrooms and communities, and our responsibility as Catholic educators directed by the social mission of the Church is to act on their behalf in the ways in which we conduct ourselves and our practice.

What do students tell us about a Preferential Option for the Poor and Vulnerable?

What was fascinating to us in our interviews with the students was the fact that discussions about educational inequity emerged from them and not initially from any questions we posed (we later added a question to our interviews that asked the students to compare their education to that of family and friends who went to other schools). As they talked about the quality of the education they were receiving, many were articulate in describing how truly vulnerable they were in schools that were not meeting their basic educational needs. Some were able to state how the opportunities being afforded to some of their peers in other schools were not being given to them. We heard from these students a conception of injustice that encompassed not only economic factors but educational factors related to expectations, curriculum, and the quality of teachers. If you recall, these are the same factors students discussed in earlier chapters as essential for their success. Now we are looking at "the other side of the coin," with students aware that inequities in their education were having a negative impact on their learning and future prospects. They understood that they were not faring well, and that if their education was being evaluated from their viewpoint, (as the bishops might suggest it should be) the system would appear to have failed many of them.

One of the ways we can respond to the call for preferential option for the poor comes in our listening to our children and acting on their behalf. Many of our students are calling out to us loudly and adamantly to be just in our work and in our interactions with them. In this section, we turn once again to the voices of urban youth who have identified particular injustices in their schools and classrooms and in their relationships with their teachers, which in many ways have rendered them vulnerable and defenseless. Let's begin by returning to Jamie's story.

As you may recall, Jamie is an eighth-grade student who had taken an entrance exam for a Catholic high school and who reported not doing as well as expected. Despite the fact that he believed himself to be capable – he's *"in the top three"* and scores *"above average"* on all of his tests – he seemed to blame himself for his poor performance on the exam – not enough sleep, a lack of focus. As the story unfolded, Jamie shared a conversation he had with his friend's father, who happened to be a principal in the suburban district that his friend attended. Jamie continued:

And the principal, not my principal, say it is probably because of the higher standards of teachers of where he [Jamie's friend] at. They say the urban area teachers teach only school materials and where they should be at a certain time. They don't teach about like steps or whatever. They teach first if you don't know multiplication they teach you that. But at Utica, they teach all kinds of things. They teach you like square root and algebra and all kinds of things that they know is on these tests. He showed us his math book and I showed him our math book and our language arts book and their books are way more advanced than ours. I mean they start off with, first they do multiplication like we do but then they go straight to algebra. We take the basics. They jump into what they need to learn. It is different tactics and stuff that teachers and students use.

We asked Jamie what all of this meant to him. He concluded his story by saying:

So I think from us being in the urban area they just teaching us different things. They [students in the suburban school] progress and learn more faster than us, probably because of the money situation or probably because we don't have that many teachers that know all the material without getting out the book.

With the help of his friend's father, Jamie came to recognize that differences in the curriculum, the level of expectations, and the quality of teaching, along with a lack of resources were the realities of his educational experience compared to those of his friend and that this may have contributed to his poor test performance.

Jamie's story made us wonder how many students in our classrooms may be confused about what is happening with their education – why they are not performing as well as their peers, or why, despite their best efforts, they just do not seem to be getting it no matter how hard they try. It made us wonder how many teachers and other significant adults are aware of students' perceptions of the types of injustice that impacts their young lives and the lives of others. How differently Jamie might have looked at himself and this situation if he had not had the opportunity to talk to this concerned adult about his performance on the entrance exam! Because this friend's dad took the time to talk to Jamie about his education, he had the opportunity to look at the situation differently. He gained an alternative explanation to the "blame the victim" mentality that so often is used by victims themselves and the educational system to explain the disparities that exist between groups of students. (We've all heard things like: *"Johnny doesn't care;" "Mary's parents are poor;" "Don's a "bad" kid;" "She's not very bright;" "He lives only with his mother;" "It's the parents. They just don't care."*)

Jamie's story offers a poignant example of how vulnerable our children can be within our educational system. He represents in many ways the voiceless and defenseless ones to whom we are challenged to give voice to by the bishops in their statement in *Economic Justice for All*. His story results from policies and social institutions that impact the poor and vulnerable in ways that make it difficult, if not impossible, for them to grow and develop. Jamie is one manifestation of the poor for which Catholic social teaching demands a preference. When we listened to Jamie's story, and to the voices of other students we talked with, it became clear that many of them are able to identify a number of injustices in their educational experiences, injustices that are a part of the experiences of our most vulnerable and needy students. Through their experiences, we are called to address these injustices in our commitment to a preferential option for the poor. Specifically, students highlighted inequities in these areas:

- Curriculum perceived as not challenging, combined with low expectations, present obstacles to equal educational opportunities and a lack of preparation for the future;

- Certain characteristics of teachers hinder student progress academically and affectively;

- A lack of resources inhibit the quality of students' education; and,

- Teachers' unexamined assumptions about students, their families, and their communities, can have a detrimental impact on students' development and success in school.

Academic Issues – Curriculum and Expectations

You may recall a seventh-grade student named Nick in an earlier chapter, who in responding to a question about the quality of education he was receiving emphatically expressed to us his opinion:

> *We in seventh grade and they started giving us multiplication. And they always talking about you all in seventh-grade, you need to start acting like you all in the grade. Well teach us like we in seventh-grade. Thank you.*

Many of the students we interviewed echoed Nick's statement expressing a desire to be academically challenged and dismay at the fact that often, at least from their perspective, many teachers held very low expectations for their academic performance and behavior. We know from our discussions in Chapter 2 that students understood the importance of high expectations and the need to be academically challenged, yet they also understood that often neither of these reflected their experience. This might be surprising to some given that it challenges a commonly held stereotype attributed to young adolescents who are often seen as apathetic and unmotivated when it comes to their studies. The students' desire for challenging curriculum and high expectations emerged as they spoke about the quality of the education they were receiving, the characteristics of caring teachers, and as they compared their school experience with those of relatives and friends attending other, more resource-rich schools. Many students expressed the conviction that they were not learning to the same degree or at the same level as some of their peers and that the reasons for this may not lie completely, if at all, with them. Students saw this as problematic and for us, it illustrates an injustice that exists in the educational experiences of many of our students. The following exchange reflects much of the conversation we heard around this theme. In this exchange, four students are comparing their experiences to those of friends and family members who attend other schools:

Evan: *My cousin, she goes to Madison Middle School. I think she knows*
          more than me because she gets homework from every single one of
          her classes. I called her up and she's always doing homework or
          studying for tests. She's over there learning all of this stuff, stuff that
          we're over here not learning nothing.

Tony: *And my cousin – she goes to Adams and we call each other every*
          day, too. They tell me what they do in school and they be asking me
          what you be doing in school, what did you learn. And I really can't
          tell them nothing because every time it's the same thing and they
          tell me different stuff every day. They work on different stuff every
          day but when they ask me I'm telling the same thing over and over
          again and they say ' Do you learn anything new?' and I'm saying,
          'No, not really.'

Jamal: *My cousin was in the fourth grade and he go to Polk schools and*
          he's learning the same stuff that we're learning in the seventh grade
          and he's only in fourth grade.

Clearly linked to this lack of a challenging learning environment is the
quality or level of expectations we hold for our students, and how if at all,
we communicate those expectations to them. We all struggle with this issue
whether we are teaching young children, adolescents or adults. How we
address the issue of expectations is influenced by our own personal
philosophies of teaching and our pedagogical knowledge base, and at times
on our stereotypes of learners based on particular characteristics. How we
respond to these issues within our own schools could have serious consequences for our students' learning and future experiences in school.

While many students may not have the right language to express their
critique of the low or inappropriate expectations that teachers sometimes
hold for their learning and their future, they are nonetheless aware that for
whatever reason, teachers do not hold them to the same standards or level
of expectations as other students within their own classrooms or other
schools. Implicit in the above conversation among the seventh-grade boys

was their understanding that what was being asked of them was less than what family and friends experienced in other schools. They realized that as a result of the injustice of low expectations they learned too little. In a conversation among a group of eighth-graders, Rebecca struck a similar chord when she expressed the following thought:

> There's a lot of kids in the eighth-grade class that are held back. They just not caring I guess. And I guess teachers must think that since they're not able to learn higher education they just teach them what fifth-graders are learning and go back to the basics.

Lack of expectations was also expressed as students discussed the level of discipline in their schools, which for many was perceived as a major obstacle to their learning. In this exchange a group of students responded to a question about why they think they are learning at a lower level than peers at another school:

James: *Because they [other schools] got more discipline. They take more charge than we do. Our school lets things happen. Like Onondaga, they have problems but they take more repercussions on it. They take more charge. We just sit back and let things happen where it can be prevented.*

Sherry: *Like in that school, if somebody act up they know what to do. We just give them another detention. That's not helping so they're going to get that every time. At Lakeview, they know how to handle the situation. They'll ask another teacher, 'What should we do about this person?' You're not going to learn nothing by being in suspension or having detention that you don't go to.*

James and Sherry seem to suggest that they expect structure and accountability in their school. They imply that a well-managed school and classroom are essential to their learning. We heard this from a number of young adolescents – an attitude once again that is not often attributed to this age group. Lack of expectations for student behavior is another example of an injustice in our classrooms, that when left unexamined or not addressed, can have a negative impact on learning.

Teacher Characteristics

It is clear from what we have heard from the students in previous chapters that a teacher knowing his or her students well is an essential element for their learning. However, some students also expressed concern that at times teachers rely on preconceived ideas about them that affect expectations for their behavior. This was most likely the basis for Rebecca's earlier comment regarding her peers who were supposed to be in the twelfth-grade. She seems to suggest that because students were being retained and appeared not to care, teachers assumed they were unable to be challenged academically. In one conversation, a group of boys were comparing their neighborhood to one of the suburban neighborhoods where a cousin attended school. This conversation was taking place in the context of a discussion of teachers' impressions of them, leading one student to conclude that teachers had lower expectations because: *"...they carry stuff from last year and they go along with things from last year. They don't really know us."*

This was a common concern as evidenced in the following conversation between two students talking about their teachers' preconceived ideas about them and how this resulted in unequal treatment. It is one of the rare occasions where students were willing or able to bring issues related to race and prejudice into their conversations:

La'Tasha: *And I think some of the teachers here, like I'm not prejudice, but I think some of them are kind of prejudice because of the way they treat us. We got a couple of White students and they get treated way different than we do.*

Marsha: *Like Isabel, she got expelled and her mom came here and then she got unexpelled. She got to do what she wanted to do and come back to school that day. I got suspended for whooping somebody and somebody else did it and I was suspended for three days. So I think some people in this school is prejudice.*

Many of the students saw reliance on preconceived notions about them as an injustice that is widespread among their teachers and a significant problem impacting their learning.

So much of what we heard from the students in previous chapters is embedded in the notion of care. Many students indicated that their teachers were very effective at communicating care for them; however some experienced a lack of care and talked about how devastating this can be. We return to this lack of care once again in this chapter since some of the students believed there was also injustice in the fact that a number of their teachers did not share the same level of care for them as teachers in other schools, schools they perceived as "better" than their own. Further, they suggested that this lack of care impacted the quality of their education. It was interesting to us that students had this perception of difference between schools in this more affective domain. While physical differences between buildings is more readily apparent, these more emotional factors would not necessarily seem to so be readily recognizable. Mical expressed the concern in these terms:

Like in Lakeview and Southlake teachers really care about their students and they take their time to teach their students and they give their students a choice and opportunities to do the work if they want to – but at our school they just don't do that.

Similarly, in another group the conversation led Shane to comment on the lack of care in his school. He had this to say:

> *Instead of having one or two teachers that care I think it matters if we have all the teachers who care and the students can respect them more. If we get more teachers who care then the students will care more and then we will have a good education because we'll get our work done. In other schools that's what it is. The teachers care more. They get down to business and they explain everything. I think that's why a lot of other schools get better grades.*

As we have seen in previous chapters, respect was a common theme in all of our interviews, particularly when discussing caring teachers and the student-teacher relationships that enhanced their learning experience. Not surprisingly, respect again surfaced in these conversations about equity as students reflected on their schooling experiences relative to others. Tanya framed the issue in these terms:

> *I think they're [the teachers] very disrespectful. If they get mad at one student they can tell them 'I don't care. I don't care if you learn or not.' So that makes the students feel like they didn't care.*

The quality of teachers, another of the justice issues these students identified, was of particular concern in one school where it seemed to the students that many of the teachers would give up pretty easily on the students. Joanne's summary of one conversation provides a synthesis of much of what we heard and the frustration that comes with not really understanding why the situation exists as it does:

> *Some teachers don't want to teach. They just give up. If something don't go their way they will get up, walk out the class, put on their coat, go jump in their car and then just leave. And then they expect everything to be just handy dandy gravy. Then you go out to the suburbs and they will work with you, and then that's what they always comparing us to. Well, when you go here there is this and there's that*

because it's teachers that care there. I mean probably they get paid more than these teachers here. I don't understand.

Observe ✐

The students have described teacher characteristics that caused a fundamental unfairness in their education. Have you observed any of the traits identified by the students in yourself or in other teachers? If so, what impact did those traits seem to have on the students?

Lack of Resources

The economic issues facing public and parochial schools are similar in that most schools lack the resources they would like to have; however, the reasons for the lack of resources, or unequal distribution of resources, are different. We are including this section, in part, to be true to the students we interviewed who identified this as an area of injustice. We also include this discussion, since as Catholic educators committed to the social mission of the Church, we have a responsibility to be concerned with the larger community as part of our own faith commitment that requires a preferential option for the poor.

If your students are like the ones we talked with, many of them are probably aware to one degree or another, of how resources are allocated. Let's look at what a few of the students shared with us. Jasmine is probably one of the students who stands out the most from all those we interviewed. She is a seventh-grade, African-American young woman who is outgoing and opinionated, a leader among her peers. She may remind you of one of the students in your class – eager to speak her mind, forceful in her delivery. She has a lot to say and she is not afraid to say it! Speaking about the quality of her education, she was, quite frankly, angry and she was eager to share her thoughts with us on the state of her schools. According to Jasmine:

The school district is just awful. I think it started as soon as the Mayor took over our schools. That's when everything just started getting messed up. He's supposed to be the head of our schools or whatever. Why we got a new sports stadium when there are no books. There are no stuff we need at school. Don't nobody want to talk about that. They always want to write about what's wrong with our schools, but they don't know. Some of these kids in here got 4.0 averages. They don't talk about all that.

This is obviously a public school case, but as concerned citizens and taxpayers, Jasmine's words should engender outrage from us as well as from the parents and the community in which this district is located. This is an area where the Church's call to a preferential option for the poor takes us beyond our own classrooms and schools and clearly demands our response to the larger community.

What was most unsettling to us, however, was the frustration that was evident in Jasmine's words and demeanor, which so clearly spoke to her vulnerability and defenselessness in light of something that was so much bigger than herself. The question for us became, how do you help students like Jasmine understand this blatant inequity while providing them the tools and strategies to combat the injustice?

Other students also expressed dismay and disappointment over the quality of their education and how that education was negatively impacted by a lack of resources. Shaundra reminded us of Jasmine. She was fired up as she spoke of her love of science and how desperately she and her peers longed for science experiments. They understood that hands-on instruction was the way to learn, but there were no science labs in Shaundra's school. In fact, in her science classroom the desks were of the type with slanted tops making experiments nearly impossible. From what she told us, it seemed that the teacher apparently made no effort to provide even simple demonstrations or experiments (not at all reflective of the many, many teachers who use their own resources to compensate for the lack of resources provided by schools). In trying to make sense of her situation, Shaundra shared with us that:

> *Everybody wants to have a science lab at this school but don't have money to do stuff like that. We don't have a lot of materials to do stuff. We don't have to waste money on buying fans. Anything creative would help us. It doesn't have to be this really big thing, anything will help us in science, cause even the littlest things matter.*

Shaundra's quick reference to the fans indicates again how some students can be keenly aware of the ways in which we decide to use the resources we do have. We asked Shaundra if not having resources kept her from learning. She responded emphatically: *"It's a big problem. Like in art. We don't do nothing. We just sit there and do homework for other classes cause we got broke up crayons and broke up chalk and stuff. Markers all dry and stuff. We have no money. We are just like so broke."* One of the things Shaundra went on to say was that students could help the situation by conducting fundraisers and the like to make up for the lack of resources impacting the quality of learning and teaching. Like Jasmine, she showed desperation and determination, yet again, the confusion of not completely understanding why the schools were in this condition, and not knowing how to act was having a detrimental effect on Shaundra and her classmates.

A few of the students commented that financial resources were distributed unequally among schools within their district. For example, Lynette suggested that: *". . . some schools have a better advantage over other schools because the school has more money and is able to do more things with students."* Brittany concurred and added: *"They [the school board] don't have the materials that other schools have. They give them better materials than they give us but I don't know the reason."* This notion of not knowing why on the part of students is very problematic. We are not certain of the impact this awareness coupled with lack of understanding has on students' self esteem, motivation, and ultimate success in school. We can only speculate at this point the negative effect that might result.

From talking with students, it was clear that many of them were aware of how the resources in their schools were distributed and whether or not the allocation was equitable. We think this awareness raises important issues for all teachers to consider. We think about the students from urban schools going to play basketball games in suburban schools and seeing vast differences in the quality of the physical resources. We think of students within the same schools, who observe differences in the resources given to athletic programs compared to academics and after school clubs and activities. We think of students within the same classrooms or grade levels who observe a difference in who goes on field trips and who is able to participate in special events. The students we spoke with told us that many of them see these differences even though the adults in their lives do not think they are capable of such astute observations. We believe this discussion of fiscal inequity speaks directly to our responsibility as Catholic educators, committed to the call to justice, to respond in a way that benefits the students – our own students if we find ourselves in situations where there is an unequal distribution of resources within our own diocese or school, but also for other students we may not know, in public and other parochial schools, who find themselves mired in schools that lack the basic resources necessary for a quality education, an education the U.S. bishops demanded in their pastoral: *Building Peace: A Pastoral Reflection on the Response to 'The Challenges of Peace* (see Chapter 1).

Observe

A question to consider – in your diocese are there differences in the allocation of resources in terms of physical plants and fiscal and human resources? Do your students see these differences? If so, how do they react to these differences? How do you react to these differences?

Examining Assumptions

Most of us are not poor and vulnerable (at least not in the way the terms are being discussed in this chapter!). So when we talk about discussing the preferential option for the poor in our schools, we may face obstacles to our recognizing and understanding the differences that exist between us and some of our students. We ourselves have confronted many of these obstacles ourselves in our work as teacher, administrator and consultant in a variety of schools. While we do not have any specific words from the students that led us to address the stereotypes, preconceived notions and unexamined assumptions that some teachers hold about their students (consciously or unconsciously), we do believe it is important for all of us to reflect on these issues in the context of our discussion of social justice in Catholic schools. If we return to the students' comments above (particularly those of Rebecca, LaTasha, Marsha, Ron, and Joanne), we hear in their voices some very troubling and profound insights into the impact teachers' preconceived notions can have on them. If we read between the lines, we wonder what the students are thinking and feeling when they hear their teachers say things like: *"I don't care if you learn or not'* or, *'They say we dumb, we don't want to learn, we just bad and stuff."* We hear in their words a cautionary note and a challenge for teachers to consider important and difficult questions, particularly when cultural and social differences exist between the teachers and their students. Questions such as:

How well do I really know my students?

On what basis do I come to know my students –

- Do I talk with them about what is important to them?

- Do I visit their homes and/or talk with their families about their hopes and dreams for their children?

- Do I seek to become more familiar with the communities and neighborhoods from which my students come, particularly if they are different from my own?

- Do I base my ideas on faculty room conversations?

- Do I hold, consciously or not, preconceived ideas about students based on their gender, ability, race, ethnicity, family structure or income?

Inquiry into these issues is difficult. They suggest relationships with students, parents, and the community that might be seen as 'beyond the call of duty,' or not realistic, or not even welcomed. And then when we get to issues raised in the last question, issues related to race, class, and gender, it becomes even more messy, uncomfortable and complex. We often avoid such questions, yet they are necessary if the injustices brought about by acting without accurate and appropriate knowledge about our students and ourselves are to be addressed for the good of the students who are entrusted to our care. This level of critical self-reflection can be hard and painful. After all, we are good people, committed to our work, and to our students. Nevertheless, we have been socialized in a country with a legacy of racism, sexism, homophobia, and classism, and this legacy, which has shaped our own prior experiences, can affect how we view and interact with others, particularly those who are different from ourselves, without our really even being aware of it.

This situation is especially problematic in the context of schools where the majority of teachers are White and middle class while the students they teach are increasingly different from them culturally and socially (while this trend is usually referred to in our public schools, statistics provided by the NCEA suggest the same trend can be seen in our nation's Catholic schools). One teacher we interviewed, Sister Monica, who was working in an urban school for the first time in her career, put it this way:

The challenge is knowing the culture because it is different. I mean two cultures, the youth and the African-American, and then maybe three cultures I should say, the culture of poverty too. So I would say that's the challenge for me because I'm White, middle class.

Mrs. Jenson and Mr. Johnson who we met in the last chapter are examples of teachers who are attempting to understand culture and the role it plays in education. We heard in their voices an appreciation for the role culture plays in education and a developing understanding of how to talk about it. Much educational research has been conducted in the last twenty years that examines the effects of the cultural mismatch that often exists between many students and their teachers. Among the findings of this body of work, misunderstandings between the school and home on a myriad of issues from behavior to schedules, expectations of students, levels of parental involvement, interaction styles, teacher efficacy, student self esteem and lack of motivation, can result from cultural differences between teachers and their students when left unexamined (refer to *"Resources for Further Reflection,"* if you would like to explore this research in more depth). Most of us who work with people who are different from ourselves address these differences one way or another. It is inevitable. Some choose to accept the challenge, embrace the diversity, and reflect on the differences and their implications directly, no matter how difficult or painful. Others choose to ignore them, an action that often inflates difficult situations and causes misunderstandings among individuals and groups to persist and fester. In the school context it is essential, even demanded by those of us committed to the social justice mission of the Church and its preferential option for the poor, to find ways to individually and collectively think about and act upon our differences, so as to use those differences as a means to enhance, rather than hinder the dignity of our students, parents and colleagues and the quality of our community.

In our work, we have had the opportunity to interview a number of teachers who work predominantly with students of color. In one school is was evident that some of the White teachers were struggling with these very issues as they examined with us the challenges and opportunities of working with their students. It is again interesting to note that we did not question teachers directly about differences that exist between them and their students. As with the students we interviewed, these discussions emerged from the teachers in response to a general question about working with students and families. This underscores the importance of this issue to teachers and students. We want to share with you some of these stories since they represent the types of challenges many of us face when working with diverse student populations. While these examples reflect issues related to racial and socio-economic status, they could just as easily be about other types of differences that exist between teachers and their students. Each of these teachers chose to teach in an urban, Catholic setting. They saw their work as a vocation, and without explicitly saying so, they were responding to the call for a preferential option for the poor.

We will begin with Mrs. Scott. Mrs. Scott is a veteran teacher of both *public and parochial schools, who chose this school: "... for the students who might not have a chance otherwise."* She acknowledged the challenges posed by being a White female working with African-American students:

> *I think the challenge without sounding racial has been the fact that I'm a White female, White middle-aged female and they're challenged by that authority figure . . . I could be wrong but I think that's what I've kind of boiled it down to, is initially they looked at me as a White lady – what does she know, she doesn't know our situation or our lives and I think there's validity to that.*

Mrs. Scott's comment about not wanting to sound racist points out how difficult it is for us to talk about these issues. However, race does matter. In many of the cities in which we work and live, racial segregation in one form or another still exists. Talking about race is taboo in many circles; it is risky business. Yet, the teachers we talked to clearly recognized that differences existed between themselves and their students, which is a first step to beginning the conversation. Mrs. Scott is assuming, and maybe rightly so, that her students have issues with White people. The legacy of racism in this country has had an impact on all of us, Black and White. It appears she recognizes this fact, and in talking to her further, her frustration with not knowing how to proceed with this knowledge is a problem for her.

Observe ✍

Do you feel any of the same discomfort Ms. Scott feels when you discuss issues of race? Do you have opportunities to talk with colleagues, particularly colleagues of color, about how race might impact the dynamics in a classroom? Have you ever thought of talking with students about race in an age/grade appropriate way?

While teachers recognized differences that existed between them and their students, occasionally they seemed to be making some assumptions about the quality of those differences. Mrs. Bryant is a veteran teacher of Catholic schools. When talking about working at this particular school she told us: *"I finally got the job I've always wanted."* In sharing her first experiences of working with diverse students, she stated that:

> *A lot of kids just don't have the same work ethic that a lot of White, middle class kids were raised with. It would never occur to me not to go to school because I just didn't feel like it, not to turn in a homework assignment because I just didn't want to. This is not in my brain, that's not wired there anyplace.*

The subtle distinction (or maybe not so subtle) Mrs. Bryant makes between the work ethic of her African-American students and White middle class students exemplifies how we often perceive difference. She seems to imply that African-American students are lazy or lack motivation, and that this is not true for White, middle class students. This raises questions related to where this perception of her students is coming from and how such a perception of students might influence a teacher's interactions with or expectations for students. It also addresses the issue of how well a teacher knows his or her students, since what might appear to be a poor work ethic, may in fact be due to some other educational or family issue unknown to the teacher.

Examples to highlight the complexities of this discussion can be found in how three teachers talked about their students' families and the impact families might have on learning. Mrs. Bryant, in explaining why her students may not do their homework, continued:

Or to be in a situation where all of my books are at my dad's house but I'm at my mom's now and my dad had a fight with his girlfriend and I had to get out of the house because it was getting loud and scary and so I ran over to my grandmothers . . . That's kind of the ordinary stuff so that kind of thinking that you have to get past that people have different sets of values from you . . . so the big challenges with the kids is that they come from a different planet!

Here the teacher suggests she thinks she understands the reasons for students not completing their work and equates those reasons with values, values that she seems to think are so different than hers that she exclaims that: *"they* [the kids] *come from a different planet!"* Viewing the students as so different, without an intimate knowledge and understanding of them, could have significant implications for our interactions with students and their families.

In another example, Mrs. Scott, in responding to a question about the opportunities and challenges of working with the school's families shared with us that:

The family structure is so different, certainly different than my upbringing, different than my family . . . we are all stuck with our families and yet that's a big issue for these kids. They're a little more sensitive to the fact that they're living with grandma and mom's not in the picture . . . so that was something for me to deal with because in the past I had more stable families.

This comment made us wonder if this teacher was suggesting that because her students came from non-traditional families, that their family experience was unstable. We all have encountered traditional two parent families who we might characterize as dysfunctional. While we do not want to be hyper-sensitive about the words we use, the fact is, the language we choose to describe our students and their actions, can influence our interactions with the students and the way in which we are perceived by them. The assumptions that we hold about each other influence our actions.

Finally, Ms. Franz, a young, idealistic teacher, committed to social justice, was drawn to work at this school because: *"... it was urban and it was Catholic."* In talking about her motivation for working with urban youth, she stated: *"I love the kids and I have so much to say and their potential, change their neighborhoods and change who they are and who their families are, that makes me committed to the school."* This teacher has the right intentions but there is a sense in Ms. Franz's statement that if we can change the students – their communities, their families, and even the students themselves – they will be more successful. This begs the question, change how? Often times the answer is to change the students to be more like me. Ms. Franz's statement highlights the challenge for all of us as to how we value difference. Do we see difference as a value to be celebrated, or do we see difference as a deficiency that needs to be 'fixed'?.

There is no question that these three women are committed and dedicated to their vocation as Catholic educators. In knowing them and their work the best interests of their students are forefront in their minds. Yet at the same time, we can see in their struggles, like so many of our own, the complexities and contradictions inherent in experiencing the cultural differences that exist between students and their teachers. These three women have chosen to work in urban schools for all the right reasons; however, they seem to be unconsciously operating from a deficit perspective that is influenced by years of socialization and which undoubtedly impacts their interactions with their students. At times it almost seems like they think their job is to 'fix' the kids and to make them more like themselves. They illustrate the dilemma faced by so many Catholic educators (including us) who commit and dedicate themselves to their students, while experiencing barriers to those efforts, often unconscious or uncritical of them.

These examples highlight another important assertion of the educational research literature regarding working with diverse students. Not unrelated to what we discussed in the last chapter about the importance of knowing our students, is the importance of knowing ourselves as well: Who are we? How has our life experience impacted our beliefs and ways of knowing about our students and about school and about the way we conduct our practice? As one teacher to whom we spoke said: *"A teacher needs to look at themselves first. What are you about? What are you really about? When you stand in front of the classroom, what do those children see?"* Conversations such as these are difficult but necessary if we are to create a system of education that is just and equitable for all its students.

Observe

Think of the diversity of students in your classroom. Do you reflect on the differences that exist in your classroom? Do you take the time to reflect on your conscious or unconscious perceptions of the variety of differences that exist in your school or classroom? What are your perceptions of the differences that exist? When you stand in front of the classroom, what do your students see?

How do we judge our response to the call to a preferential option for the poor & vulnerable?

It goes without saying that as teachers we are committed to all of our students, particularly those with the most need, the ones who are the most vulnerable. The preferential option for the poor is deeply engrained in our mission and in our vocation as Catholic educators. In this chapter we had the privilege of listening to students, many of whom are probably very similar to those in your own classrooms, who believe their education is being compromised by inequities that exist in our schools. They helped us to define justice in very broad terms and in terms that are meaningful to them and to their success in school. Whether we teach the very young or the adolescent, or students somewhere in between, we know that they are keenly aware of what is fair and what is right. In the simplest way that is what we are talking about here – our preferential option for children for whom their educational experience is neither fair nor right and who have no voice or power to change it. The students we interviewed highlight the unfairness that at times manifests itself in low expectations, weak curricula, poor teaching, and lack of resources. The students' perspectives give us an opportunity to critically examine our practices in light of how we meet the needs of all of our students. We have also listened to teachers who shared with us their struggles and challenges as they work with diverse students. These experiences give us an opportunity to critically examine the norms, values, and beliefs that impact our interactions with children, particularly those who are different from ourselves.

For those of us working directly with the poor in all its manifestations, we can be almost certain that these students experience injustice on a daily basis. The students' awareness of injustice raises questions for us in terms of how to address this awareness and understanding with students. We fear that once identified, if this awareness goes unexamined, the students could suffer from the consequences of confusion and misunderstanding. As Catholic educators committed to social justice we are all responsible for what happens in our schools, and so our commitment to justice, to responding to those with the most need, is a collective responsibility as well as an individual one. We all need to be aware that our students do understand that injustice exists around them, not only in their neighborhoods and cities, but also in their schools and classrooms. We need to find out what they know and understand, and then help them make sense out of the situation so they are never tempted to blame themselves needlessly. We need to provide students developmentally appropriate ways of addressing situations they perceive to be unjust, individually and collectively, with their peers and with us, so that they can see they have the power to bring about positive change.

We also have a responsibility to those students who have little or no awareness of or experience with the injustices that exist all around them. We need to think about how do we help our students who are from privileged backgrounds come to see and understand the benefits of that privilege. Once identified, we need to provide students a way to use their privilege to commit themselves to transforming the social structures that perpetuate the various forms of poverty and inequity.

Discussion

Throughout this chapter we have once again taken time to *observe* aspects of our own teaching practice and the experiences of students that help us better understand the Church's call to a preferential option for the poor. As in previous chapters, we now invite you to follow Pope John XXIII's urging to judge the ways in which we are effective in our response to the Church's and our students' call to a preferential option for the poor. Teachers might begin by sharing some of their observations of how a preferential option for the poor is reflected in their own vocations, classrooms and in their school as a whole. It is important to recognize where we are already responding to this call to justice. A second step might be, as in previous chapters, to talk about any surprises we heard from the Church and from the students quoted in this chapter. You may also decide to use some of the following questions as a starting point to tackle the more difficult task of sharing candidly the ways in which you can deepen your shared commitment to justice in your school and make sure that you regularly examine how your actions respond to the Church's call for a preferential option for the poor.

1. Sharing our observations (be as specific as possible):
   - In my classroom, how do I live or make evident a preferential option for the poor?
   - How do I respond to the call for a preferential option for the poor in listening to these students' as they relate their understanding of inequity?

- How might students interpret my attitudes and practices toward the most vulnerable in my class and in my community?

- How do I respond to my own students who may perceive injustices in our school and in our classroom and in my interactions with them?

2. Judging our whole school's response to a preferential option for the poor: Discuss the same questions above, but consider the school as a whole during your discussion.

3. As I (we) listened to the Church and the students in this chapter, what did they say that surprised me?

4. Deepening our shared commitments

- How might I, individually and in collaboration with my colleagues, insure that my classroom and our school are equitable for all students? Beyond my school and classroom?

- Here we might reflect on expectations from a different perspective than we did in earlier chapters: Do I hold the same expectations for all students? Do I lower expectations for some students based on my perceptions of them? Do I differentiate my expectations based on students' individual differences? If I should, how do I differentiate my instruction to meet the needs of all of the students? Are my expectations high enough, challenging enough? Are my expectations of my students influenced in any way, consciously or unconsciously, by what I know or think about individual students?

- Earlier in this chapter we met LaTasha and Marsha who broached the subject of prejudice on the part of teachers toward students. This can be a difficult situation to handle with students of any age, but as these two young women pointed out to us, students do have these beliefs, whether justified or not. If LaTasha and Marsha were talking about someone in my school, how would I/we react to this exchange? How might I/we help the students understand their perceptions and deal with them in honest and respectful ways? How might I talk with my colleagues about students' perceptions of prejudice among the faculty?

- In thinking about assumptions regarding my students, their families and their communities:

- Do I/we recognize and talk about the existence of racial, cultural and social differences with colleagues and students in areas like values, norms, child-rearing practices, communication styles, and interaction patterns?

- Do I/we place value judgments on these differences – mine are better than yours? How might my/our ideas about the differences that exist between me/us and our students and their families impact the way I/we think about/interact with students and families?

- Do I/we value the diversity our students and families bring to our schools and classrooms? How do I/we communicate that the diversity is valued and honored?

- Do I/we feel the need to 'change' my/our students to be 'more like me/us' in order for them to be successful?

- How do I/we use the diversity present in our classrooms and schools to enrich the lives of all the members of the school community?

126

CHAPTER FIVE

They Call Us to Act

" If Catholic education and formation fail to communicate our social tradition, they are not fully Catholic."

—USCCB, *Sharing Catholic Social Teaching:
Challenges and Directions*

AT THE BEGINNING OF CHAPTER 1, WE REFLECTED ON TEACHING as a call from God to serve through our work with children. We asked ourselves why God chose us and what he called us to do. Now that we have listened to the voices of our students and heard again the teachings of the Church, we may see more clearly that, in fact, our call to teaching is a call to justice. The new question then is: What does it mean to accept this call to be just from God, the Church, and our students? How do we protect the dignity of individuals, create community, and ensure equity in our work as teachers?

To accept the call to justice is to *act*. Throughout this book we have been guided by the words of Pope John XXIII who urged all people to translate social doctrine into reality. He laid out a simple, but powerful process for us – observe, judge, act. The Bishops have mandated that Catholic social teaching be placed at the center of our work in schools, parishes, and Catholic life. In fact, in speaking about Catholic education, their task force stated that every diocese should incorporate Catholic social teaching in their standards for in-service training of teachers and in their curriculum guidelines. But these have remained elusive goals. We believe that by connecting the complexities of social teaching to John XXIII's simple process, teachers and schools can put in place a structure that will allow us to make a commitment to justice that is part of the very fabric of life in our Catholic schools. In the previous chapters of this book, you have already done important work to fulfill John XXIII's hopes for us as Catholics by observing and judging your classrooms and schools.

In this chapter we have adapted the formula "Observe, Judge, Act" into a model of school practice that responds to our mission, while making it easier for us to maintain our focus on justice as a core principle guiding all the decisions we make in our schools (see Figure 1).

Figure 1: Observe, Judge and Act: Cycle of Professional Practice

At the core of the model and our mission as Catholic educators is the call to justice we have heard from the Church and from our students, helping us to remember that their call is the reason for our work. That call is focused on three key themes that underlie our work: the dignity of the individual person, community, and a preferential option for the poor or equity. In schools, these themes are closely linked to the everyday decisions that involve the content of the curriculum, our teaching practices and strategies, the climate of our classrooms and school, our relationships with our students and their families. When we are working in that "circle," we are involved in the hard everyday work of teaching. And it is in this sphere of activity that we can easily lose our attention on the principles of justice because of the urgency of our continual decisions as teachers. In order to maintain our commitment to justice, this framework wraps all of our work in cycles of observing, judging, and acting as we work to teach for equity and justice.

We understand that no two teachers or schools are alike as they begin to move forward in their commitment to justice. Now that you have engaged in observing and judging your own school's needs, action steps will be highly individualized. One thing we are sure of is that wherever you are now, it can be rewarding to develop action plans that will make substantive differences in the quality of justice in your classrooms and schools. Whatever the starting point, if we hold ourselves accountable to ongoing cycles of observing, judging, and acting, it will be much easier to maintain our focus on justice. In the rest of this chapter, we will highlight certain areas of our work that provide opportunities for us to begin or to advance our work on justice. These may be starting places for you and/or your colleagues – or they may serve as a catalyst for you as you create your own direction for action.

Listening to Our Students

We are certain that by now you know how much we have come to value listening to our students. We began the introduction to this book with a quote from a young man who made it clear why we should listen to students: *"I think you should ask the kids because they do know more than you think they know."* Interviewing nearly 300 young people has certainly caused us to reflect on our work as teachers and wonder how well and how thoughtfully we really listened to our students when we were in elementary and middle school classrooms. One of our greatest hopes is that when people read our work, or listen to us present our research, they will be inspired to go back to their own classrooms and listen carefully to their own students in thoughtful and planned ways (if they're not already doing so). We sincerely believe that as we continually strive to become better teachers that we need to listen to the perspectives of students and incorporate those perspectives into our practice. Our research has taught us that their insights into effective teaching practices, the student-teacher relationship, and the classroom environment confirm the significance of the various theories and strategies that provide the foundations of our practice. Further, they give us a different lens through which to view our role as teachers for equity and justice. And in the spirit of this text, careful listening is yet another way to honor and respect students' dignity as human persons.

And so we think that one of the first steps teachers can take in responding to their reading of this text is to find ways to really listen to students in genuine, meaningful and focused ways. We are not suggesting that teachers do not listen to their students already. What we are suggesting is that we develop a habit or disposition toward listening that is systematic, planned, and implemented. The benefits of listening to our students, really listening, are innumerable to us and to them. As we talked with students and asked their opinions on various issues, you could see in their eyes and in their actions (and sometimes in their expressed disbelief at the fact that we wanted to know their opinions at all!) the sense of pride they felt in being asked about their beliefs and ideas. Nel Noddings, to whom we introduced you Chapter 2, speaks to the importance of listening to students as she discusses caring relations as the foundation for pedagogical practice. She writes:

> *First, as we listen to our students, we gain their trust and, in an ongoing relation of care and trust, it is more likely that students will accept what we try to teach. They will not see our efforts as 'interference' but, rather, as cooperative work proceeding from the integrity of the relation. Second, as we engage our students in dialogue, we learn about their needs, working habits, interests, and talents. We gain important ideas from them about how to build our lessons and plan for their individual progress. Finally, as we acquire knowledge about our students' needs and realize how much more than the standard curriculum is needed, we are inspired to increase our own competence. (Noddings, 2005, 4-5)*

Noddings speaks to many of the same issues the students have brought up throughout the previous chapters. Listening to students invariably acknowledges their dignity; builds, nurtures and strengthens community; and helps us meet the varied needs of our students, particularly those who are the most vulnerable.

Many of you are probably already doing this in one way or another. We would suggest that it is important for individual teachers and teams of teachers to reflect on how to incorporate students' voices into your class-rooms and schools in systematic ways. The questions you ask, and the means by which you ask them, will vary according to your school contexts. When we began interviewing students we had particular questions we asked initially based on our work with a particular group of teachers (for example, what does it mean to get a good education? Are you receiving a good educa-tion at your school? Think of a teacher in whose classroom you learned a lot. What was it about that teacher that helped you learn?). As the nature of our work changed, so did some of the questions. What you want to know and why you want to know it will undoubtedly guide the questions you ask and the context in which you ask them. One group of teachers we worked with decided to invite eighth grade students regularly to one of their faculty weekly team meetings to discuss issues related to curriculum planning and classroom management. Teachers at another school who were engaged in action research projects (which we will discuss later in this chapter) decid-ed that one of their data sources would be interviews with students. Some teachers interviewed their own students for the project, while other teachers asked colleagues to interview their students in order not to limit what the students might say. We have also heard of teachers who teach interviewing skills to their students as part of the language arts curriculum, and then have students interview each other about important issues related to the class-room or the school. The important thing to consider in all of this is that young children and adolescents can become trusted and respected partners in their education and their involvement need not be limited to planning a dance or decorating a hallway. Our work leads us to believe that students have a role to play in larger issues – improving teaching and learning, teacher-student relationships, school-wide activities and the like.

Listening to students is a way of actualizing the *"observe, judge, act"* process that we advocate in this text. As we listen to the students, we are observing their needs, their concerns, their values, their culture, their hopes and dreams. We are searching for what serves to enhance as well as what diminishes those hopes and dreams. We then make decisions based on our evaluation of what we have observed, making judgments about our students, ourselves, and our practice. To fully honor and acknowledge our students' voices, it is imperative then that we act. The challenge for us becomes how can we take the students' perspectives, ideas, and desires, and incorporate them in meaningful ways in our everyday planning and practice. To act in this way honors our students' dignity and builds community in our classrooms and schools.

Teacher Collaboration

Over the past ten years or more, the idea of teachers working together has become a core principle of school improvement efforts. The strategies have had a variety of names – professional learning communities, critical friends groups, leadership teams, grade level teams, etc. – but the basic premise is quite simple. In order to improve the quality of education in our schools, teachers need to open their classroom doors and begin to share their knowledge and expertise. They need to study together, share student work, compare notes, collaborate on planning, and analyze common data. They need to take responsibility for playing a leadership role in educating the children in their schools. In short, many of the best minds in education have urged teachers to build community in just the way that the Church and our students have described it in the first chapters of this book. In spite of this repeated urging, in many schools teachers remain isolated in their classrooms. This book has been written with the expectation that two or more teachers have joined together to read and discuss it. That is all that is needed to begin working with your colleagues to make the call to justice a central part of teacher collaboration in your school. After all, we cannot expect our schools to become communities if we do not have a community process at the center of our work as the adults in the school.

The first step in teacher collaboration, of course, is to make a judgment about how much you already collaborate in your school. Some of you may find that your school still operates on the closed-door approach and that little systematic professional discussion happens on a regular basis. This was true in most of the schools we have worked in over the years. Time and again teachers were most excited about the chance to simply TALK to each other about professional matters. If that is the case in your situation, you may do just what the teachers in the introduction of this book did – decide that a few of you will meet together to discuss your ideas and to talk seriously about how you can make justice real in your classrooms. It is wise to connect with your principal and engage him/her in supporting your efforts to discuss your professional practice (he or she may even buy you the book!). Little by little your enthusiasm for the positive impact such collaboration has on your work will become evident, and you can invite others to join you. In many schools, this is exactly how a collaborative community begins. This is, in fact, how the approach to professional development known as Critical Friends began. The National School Reform Faculty has excellent, teacher-friendly resources on line (see "Resources for Further Reflection") that provide discussion techniques (known as "protocols") to guide your study together to make your work more effective and satisfying.

Other schools may already have grade level meetings or a substantive faculty forum of some type. If so, it might be helpful to have an honest discussion about how much you actually discuss professional practice in those meetings. In our own experience, often they are a time to discuss problems with individual students (or parents) or to cover the logistics of school life. If that is the case, these meetings do not fulfill their potential as a powerful professional tool that leads to continuous improvement in the education of our children. We know a number of schools that decided to elevate the work in grade level meetings to create a professional learning community like those described by Richard Dufour and Robert Eaker (see *"Resources for Further Reflection"*). Such learning communities hold themselves accountable to a series of simple questions that guide their work together.

No matter how effective your meetings already are, you may be able to make a commitment that at every session, you will discuss some aspect of how justice becomes real in your classrooms or school. Your guiding questions may be something like these:

- In what ways are we modeling or practicing Catholic social teaching in our classrooms (observe)?

- How do we know if it is working (judge)?

- What can we do to make it work better (act)?

As you make such questions a regular part of your agenda, you will find that your discussion will deepen and will begin to affect many aspects of your professional practice. Soon this dialogue can expand beyond individual discussion groups or grade level meetings and become a regular part of faculty meetings and other professional development activities.

The ultimate goal of teacher collaboration is to change the very culture of the school. We believe that a focus on justice will have a profound effect on the education that students receive and on the quality of life in the school. If we want to have truly great Catholic schools, every teacher in the school will see him/herself as a leader, responsible for excellence in every aspect of professional work with children. We in Catholic schools have a particular opportunity to distinguish ourselves in this way, because we are working within the context of Catholic social teaching that not only encourages us, but requires us to incorporate dignity, community, and equity into the nature of our work. Community takes on new meaning if we extend it to the high level professional collaboration that is possible. One school we worked in developed a *"Professional Code of Conduct"* for their teachers that incorporated specific standards the teachers set for themselves, many of them responding to issues of justice. Some schools may even decide to join with other elementary schools, with area high schools or with Catholic colleges or universities to expand the dialogue on how we can create just communities of learners. If a faculty commits to increasing collaboration and professional dialogue in this way, they will find many resources that can support their efforts (see *"Resources for Further Reflection"*).

Class Meetings & Other School Rituals

Sometimes Catholic schools assume that by our very nature we are caring communities and that the students will somehow just know that. Particularly with the academic demands placed on schools today from high stakes testing and accountability measures, some schools worry that they do not have the time for some of the activities and rituals that build community within the school. Perhaps the most fundamental source of community building is the morning meeting. The Responsive Classroom (see *"Resources for Further Reflection"*) is one approach that we have seen transform the quality of the social and academic environment in a number of schools. By following simple meeting procedures, children develop cooperation, empathy, caring, and responsibility that help them to join with their teacher in creating a real community. The morning meeting can become the important first opportunity to really get to know our students and for them to know each other. A principal in one school we know expanded the morning meeting to have primary and middle grades division meetings on a regular basis with a planned structure that he led where students could discuss important school-wide issues that mattered to them.

An important extension of the morning meeting for young adolescents in middle school is an advisory program. Advisory is a special program that is designed to meet the needs and interests of students by linking an adult to a group of 12–15 students who meet on a regular basis to discuss issues of importance to their emerging adolescence as well as their academic performance. It is a way for us to translate our attitude of caring into action. The National Middle School Association provides excellent resources on the research that supports the advisory concept and tools that make advisory successful (see *"Resources for Further Reflection"*). Advisory takes many different forms in schools, but successful programs display certain essential characteristics:

- Every student is known well by the adult advisor and feels that the advisor will advocate for his/her best interest.

- Every student develops a sense of community and safety with the peer group that is together in advisory.

- The advisory focuses on ensuring success academically, socially, and personally for each student.

- The advisory enhances communication between the school and the home.

- The advisory engages teachers and students in meaningful dialogue about "real" life issues that matter to the students.

- The advisory meets regularly and for a long enough time to allow for meaningful dialogue and community-building.

We know that the middle school years are a time when too many students turn off to school or begin to make poor choices. We heard in the students' voices many of their concerns that could be addressed through an effective advisory program.

Every year we have a new opportunity to begin to create a more positive school culture. The Responsive Classroom encourages teachers to think carefully about the first six weeks of school, that time when the tone of the classroom and of the school year is set and we chart a course for the outcomes we hope to achieve. We worked in one school whose social culture was in deep trouble; student behavior was poor and teacher morale was low. A group of teachers started a program they called "Great Start." They developed activities that occurred in every classroom during the first few weeks of school. Students worked to develop rules with consequences that made sense to them; they developed a job plan to keep their classrooms safe and pleasant; they invented routines that would make the day work better for them; they talked about celebrations they could share when things went well in their classroom. The school created teams that engaged in cooperative activities that built community across grade levels. They even changed their school mascot from the Tigers to the Peaceful Pandas and got tee shirts for the students. The following school year was a positive experience for all, and those Great Start traditions have been part of the school for more than ten years.

Curriculum & Instruction

The structures that we create through class meetings and other school rituals for our students, of course, are closely connected to the academic time in which students are engaged most of the day. The students you heard in the previous chapters have already provided you with insights into academic experiences that promote their dignity as persons, create community, and ensure equity. You probably noticed that many of their comments about what helps them to learn sounded like a list of teaching strategies from an education textbook: hands-on learning; academic choices; scaffolding learning; meaningful content; avoiding worksheets; group activities; learning rooted in their own questions; and so on. But the students we interviewed indicated that often these were not the strategies they experienced in their classrooms, which made us wonder: "Why not?" Teachers certainly want their students to learn and to "love school," and yet too frequently neither happens to the extent we hope it will. Perhaps grounding our teaching practice in the call to justice from the Church and our students may help us solve this dilemma.

As we said earlier, once the school year begins all of us are focused on daily lesson plans and student outcomes that are the lifeblood of the school day. Efficiency has become the driving force in education and we are often compelled to return to traditional methods that work quickly, but perhaps not effectively given what we now know about learning and about justice. Perhaps we need a double set of questions to guide our planning of curriculum and instruction:

Curriculum and Instruction (DuFour and Eaker, 2004)	The Call to Justice
What do I want the children to learn?	How will my knowledge of the children I teach impact the content of their learning?
How will they learn it best?	What strategies will promote their individual dignity and community?
How will I know if they have learned it?	How can I assess their learning in ways that are just to all students?

This set of questions would lead to planning that might look very different from the textbooks that we follow in our classrooms, leading us to adapt material in new ways that might correspond more closely to what we have heard from students in this book.

When we begin to plan in this way, one of the most powerful assets we can develop is a commitment to *"Culturally Responsive Teaching"* that is rooted in deep knowledge of the students we teach. This approach does not create a new curriculum; rather it takes the knowledge and skills that students need for the future, connecting it to the prior knowledge and experiences of the students and an understanding of their performance styles in our classrooms. Culture is not only defined by the students' national or ethnic background, but by a variety of other economic, social, and geographic factors. When a teacher or a school commits to culturally responsive teaching, they commit to a focus on building upon the students' strengths as persons and as learners.

Geneva Gay (2000) has outlined principles to guide our efforts to implement culturally responsive teaching. These principles correspond closely to the principles of social justice that we have considered in the previous chapters and to the questions we outlined in the chart above:

- **Culturally responsive teachers learn** about the cultural heritage of their students. They go beyond the more easily seen aspects of culture (food, holidays, etc.) and learn about the important interpersonal norms, family values, learning styles, use of language, and verbal and nonverbal communication styles that are influenced by culture and that may be different from their own.

- **Culturally responsive teachers affirm** cultural heritage in their choices of course content and learning strategies, in their choice of activities and rituals in the classroom, and in their interactions with families. Literature and other classroom materials include many cultural perspectives.

- **Culturally responsive teachers respect** the dignity of the whole child, thinking deeply about the culturally-rooted aspects of the intellectual, social, and emotional life of the child. They are concerned not only with academic achievement but with maintaining the cultural identity of the child.

- **Culturally responsive teachers use** teaching and assessment strategies that respect the culturally based strengths of the child. They help students understand how to evaluate their own work and give them opportunities to do so.

- **Culturally responsive teachers communicate** their concern that students become successful students and good human beings who are responsible not only for themselves but for the common good. They empower students to have confidence in their abilities and in the strengths they bring to the school from their homes and families.

- **Culturally responsive teachers identify** the existing strengths of individual students and help them to recognize and develop those strengths. They celebrate many different kinds of accomplishments in their classrooms.

Catholic schools committed to social justice can make culturally responsive teaching an essential part of their mission. Study and implementation of this essential aspect of teaching can be another step in enhancing our practice of justice in our schools (see *"Resources for Further Reflection"*).

Service Learning

Picking up trash on a riverbank is service. Studying water samples under a microscope is learning. When science students collect and analyze water samples, document the results and present findings to a local pollution control agency – that's service learning. (Courtesy of the National Youth Leadership Council)

The students we interviewed indicated their desire to be of service to others, whether it was in their school or in the community. Some students also suggested that service activities had a positive impact on their learning. The students were responding to a teacher who often included service learning in his instruction. Service Learning is a teaching strategy that enhances learning by engaging students in meaningful service to their schools and communities. At all grade levels, students are able to apply academic skills while solving real-world problems. In Catholic schools, we have the added dimension of framing service as an experience or extension of one's faith in response to particular social, political or economic needs. From this perspective, service learning provides teachers and students the opportunity to make concrete their commitment to justice – to human dignity, the community, and to the poor and vulnerable. It provides students the chance to collaborate with each other, their teachers and their communities in meaningful and important ways. In this way, service learning is a tool or strategy for building community, both within the classroom and school, and beyond.

It is important to distinguish service learning from community service. Many, if not all of our schools, engage in some type of community service on a regular basis whether through food drives, working in food kitchens, or collecting money to buy books for children as part of disaster relief projects. Service is an essential aspect of our identity as Catholic schools. It is central to our mission. What distinguishes service learning from community service is the integration of the service activity with standards, learning objectives, academic skills and content and the requirement that students engage in reflection activities on their service experience. According to the National Council for the Social Studies (2000), quality service learning activities: (1) encourage student and community input in the design of the experience; (2) integrate meaningful service with essential course content; (3) require reflection on the service experience making connections between the experience and democratic values and citizenship (and for us in Catholic schools, connections to Catholic social teaching); and (4) focus on change rather than charity giving students the chance to question the status quo and look for new ways to create just and equitable situations.

There are many benefits of implementing service learning for students, teachers, and their communities for us to consider. In our experience, and in the experiences of some of the students we interviewed, service learning provides relevant and meaningful learning activities for students while at the same time connecting them with the larger community. From an academic perspective, service learning can enhance critical thinking and problem solving skills while at the same time meeting national, state and diocesan standards and learning outcomes. From a faith perspective, service learning is a tangible means of incorporating Catholic social teaching into the curriculum. Another benefit of this approach is that it can increase students' and teachers' awareness of their communities, its problems and unmet needs, and the agencies and institutions involved in meeting those needs. Through service learning, students connect with real people and real institutions working for justice. Finally, service learning can enhance the development of democratic values and attitudes in students, and for those of us in Catholic schools, it can build their commitment to social justice. Students experience first hand the injustices that exist in our communities and develop knowledge of such concepts as diversity, justice, equality and the common good.

The possibilities for service learning projects are endless. Sometimes teachers develop them individually or as a team. Other times, teachers elicit students' ideas for projects related to what they are learning. Here are a few examples to consider (these examples are taken from the National Youth Leadership Council – see *"References for Further Reflection"*).

A FOURTH GRADE CLASS IS STUDYING THE DECLARATION ON the Rights of the Child and the Universal Declaration of Human Rights. The teacher had the group brainstorm ideas, identify projects, and conduct related research. The results of the brainstorming included students creating a presentation on the Rights of the Child that was given at City Hall and the governor's mansion. The students organized and participated in a peace site rededication and a peace prize festival. They also wrote and performed a play about child labor. After they performed the play for the local school board, the board agreed that the district would not buy soccer balls made by child labor. Through this experience the students worked on public speaking, interviewing and photography skills. They regularly discussed what they learned, wrote in their journals, and analyzed related issues. In Catholic schools, they would have also addressed issues related to human dignity clearly related to Catholic social teaching's emphasis on economic and social injustices.

IN AN EIGHT-GRADE SCIENCE CLASS, STUDENTS WERE DISCUSSING the growing threat of buckthorn – a tall non-native shrub that spreads aggressively forcing out local flora including tree saplings. Students did an issue analysis, community education program and cleanup projects. The students divided themselves into action groups to research and respond to the problem, with different groups focusing on educating elementary students, conducting public surveys, contacting media outlets, and designing a brochure for a river bluff specialist. In the spring, the students helped the county Parks Department with a buckthorn removal project. Besides the many academic and social skills embedded in this project, the experience could also be seen as a response to another of the U. S. Bishops themes of Catholic social teaching – Stewardship of God's Creation.

Finally, a kindergarten example (lest we think this doesn't apply to the young child). In studying the letter "Q," the teacher read children's books about quilts, both fiction and nonfiction, to give them the historical and cultural backgrounds on the origins of quilts. They reflected on how quilts relate to family traditions and discussed the emotional and physical comfort a quilt can provide. The children then created a quilt to comfort a baby residing in a nearby shelter. When the quilt squares were completed and stitched together, each child took the quilt home where parents and students wrote and drew their thoughts and impressions in a journal that accompanied the quilt. The process culminated when the baby and mother visited the classroom and received the quilt. If you think about it, the three bedrock principles on which this book has focused – human dignity, community, and a preferential option for the poor – are all addressed in this activity for the very young in our schools.

Many of you may already be incorporating service learning in your curriculum. If you are not already connecting this work to Catholic social teaching, you might begin to plan activities in such a way that you introduce your students to this rich body of Church teaching. If your emphasis up to now has been on community service, you might now begin to think about how you could connect service activities more explicitly with the curriculum you are teaching and to the social teaching of the Church. In any event, service learning provides teachers in Catholic schools the opportunity to integrate Catholic social teaching into the curriculum in meaningful and relevant ways, and it provides students the chance to join us in the process of observing, judging, and acting.

Collaboration with Families

Classroom teachers all agree that the home deeply affects our work with children and research confirms that strong, positive connections between home and school promote success for students. Often we use the term parent "involvement" to describe those positive home-school ties. We sometimes think that parents who really care about their children's education are the ones who are present in the school for parent meetings, conferences, helping with school activities, etc. We are dismayed by parents who seem to be disengaged from the school and we often assume it means that they do not care about their child's education. Our relationships with families call for us to look for new ways to support the dignity of the individual, to build community, and to ensure equity. We need to look more deeply at opportunities to create a school culture that encourages more and more parents to join with us fully in a partnership that benefits the children in our schools.

The most important step we can take to enhance that partnership is to respect the dignity of the individual family in the same way that we have examined respecting the dignity of the individual child. That begins with knowing well the families in our school. Not all families are alike. Some children have the traditional two parents. Some divide their time between two households. Some children live with relatives other than their parents. Some children live in foster homes. Some children live with two moms or two dads. We need to know about the financial circumstances of our families, as well as the work and family demands that affect their lives. We need to know about the community in which they live. The one common denominator is that the adults in our students' lives want the best for their children. We need to look with deep respect at the circumstances that surround life for the families in our schools and try to build on the strengths they bring to the partnership of educating their children.

Each classroom and the school as a whole can assess whether or not they communicate a positive culture of respect and care to families. It is wise to keep in mind that many parents have not had positive school experiences themselves. They may feel inadequate and even intimidated in their contacts with teachers and administrators. They may not understand the policies and procedures that we take for granted as educators and they may be fearful of making a mistake. If they were not highly successful in school, they may be afraid to be too involved in their child's schoolwork.

When they hear from the school, they may assume that it means trouble of some kind. These feelings and attitudes are powerful and it takes a genuine commitment to building community to reassure parents that we are truly their partners.

Change probably begins most easily right in the child's classroom. In our experience, teachers who reach out to families at the very beginning of the year to set a positive classroom climate have the most success with parents. As part of the Great Start program we mentioned earlier in this chapter, teachers agreed to make contact with every family early in the school year. They did not wait for "back to school night" when they would greet all the parents en masse. Instead, they agreed to contact every family in some more personal way before the school year even got started. Many made phone calls to each family, some sent personalized notes, a few even made visits to the children's homes. But the message was clear: I want to welcome you and your child to my classroom. I want you to get to know me, and I want to begin to know you and your child. And most importantly, I am happy to learn from you and to work with you to ensure that your child has a wonderful year. These teachers got off on a good foot with the parents, and it paid dividends throughout the year.

Warm, positive communication with parents can thaw the chill that often exists between home and school. What we communicate (positive things as well as negative), when we communicate (regularly and not just at report card time), and how we communicate (respectfully and genuinely) should be carefully considered. We know one school where teachers printed postcards that said: "Good News from Ms. _____." They would jot down short notes about a particular child and mail it home – and kept track to make sure that all families got one occasionally. Class newsletters are valuable, too, especially when they inform families of what the children are doing in their work and how families can support their children. One teacher we know provided a list of library books they could read to their children for each unit, "family field trips" they might want to take to support the child's learning, and even simple math games they could play to reinforce the concepts they were learning in school (and the children helped to create the newsletter using technology). In short, all of these examples show communication that is encouraging and non-threatening to parents.

Of course, one of the most important contacts between home and school is the parent-teacher conference. In her anecdotal study of family-teacher relationships, Sara Lawrence-Lightfoot (2003) refers to the conference as the *"essential conversation."* Her interviews with parents and teachers reveal that when we look carefully at individual conferences, we begin to see patterns that provide insight into the school culture in general. She identified the ways in which individual and family history, as well as larger cultural attitudes, influence the outcome of conferences. She cautions us to note that the practices we follow in conducting conferences can have a profound impact on the quality of the interaction. And finally, she emphasizes that the conference, which we accept as one of the common school "routines," is actually something of a mine-field where serious damage can be done to the relationship between home and school.

This is another area for study. Perhaps the most significant thing a teacher or school can do to respond to these issues, is to begin to see parent conferences as an important opportunity for parents, teachers, and children to help each other understand the child better and to share goals and action steps. Many schools have begun to include students in the conference, thus creating a real sense of the partnership among the child, the family, and the teacher. In student-led conferences, the students are prepared to reflect on their own work, evaluate their efforts, articulate goals, and seek support from their families to achieve their goals. A simple shift in timing so that conferences do not have to correspond with "report card pickup" can allow for greater time and preparation and can make a huge difference in the quality of the interaction between families and schools.

Depending on the particular needs of a school community, creating a parent center can also have a positive impact on relations with parents. By creating a special, inviting room where parents can gather to have informal conversations, to work on school-related projects or to get information from the school, parents may feel more welcome in the school. Some schools use a parent center to provide educational opportunities for parents. In a number of schools, we saw teachers who invited parents to participate in literature circles or writing workshops (activities that they used with children) with great success. Family members who had been embarrassed about their own academic limitations suddenly were having fun at school and found that they had things to contribute that they had not realized. When they shared their writing with their children, the children, the parents and the school benefited. They went on to read books about parenting and to collaborate with each other to benefit all the children in the school.

The opportunities to view family collaboration through the lens of social justice are unlimited if we use creative thinking. If we see our work as involving a community that extends outside the school to families, extended families, parishes and neighborhoods, we can respond to the call to justice in much more tangible ways. We will talk in the next section about action research and the area of family collaboration is an excellent place to implement projects to evaluate the impact our work has on families.

Action Research

As teachers we are involved in inquiry on a daily basis. We are constantly asking questions, diagnosing problems, trying different interventions, and determining if what we have done is having the intended effect, and if it is not, deciding what to do differently. Action research, sometimes called teacher research, takes the inquiry we are already doing and turns it into a more systematic process. This type of inquiry, conducted by teachers, principals, school counselors, or other stakeholders in the teaching/learning environment, gathers information about the ways that particular schools operate, how instruction occurs, and how well students learn. In extending the framework we have used in this book, action research provides teachers an important way to observe, judge and act in their particular setting. In this section we would like to introduce you to action research as one way of reflecting on your practice, particularly in those areas that have been highlighted throughout our discussion of answering the call to justice.

If you have worked on a master's degree you no doubt have taken an (oftentimes dreaded) educational research methods course. Usually these classes focus on traditional types of research conducted by university folks and others who swoop into schools, gather data, and write their articles required for tenure. We are not making a value judgment here about this type of research (particularly since we do this type of work ourselves!), but we do want to distinguish it from the type of research teachers do in their own classrooms. Action research is about developing an interest in professional inquiry, that is, encouraging ourselves to be continuous learners who reflect regularly on our daily routines. Action research is about developing a professional disposition toward inquiry that is, encouraging teachers to be continuous learners and to assume a reflective stance in their daily routines. In addition, engaging in action research individually and in collaboration with others can help us seek to make progress on school-wide priorities while building a professional culture within our schools.

The steps in the process of conducting action research are similar to those of the scientific method we teach our elementary students. Let us briefly look at these stages with a few examples of how this works in schools:

1. Selecting a Focus:

In this first step, teacher researchers identify a topic by asking the question: *"What element(s) of our practice or what aspect of student learning do we wish to investigate or learn more about?"* The focus here could be on an individual student, group of students, an entire class, team of teachers, or it could be school wide. Topics might include particular learning strategies, classroom management, student-teacher relationships, or classroom/school climate. Whatever the topic, it should be within your locus of control, something you feel passionate about, and something you would like to change or improve. Engaging in this step involves *observation* of the current situation in order to assess areas for which questions can be raised.

2. Identifying Research Questions:

Once a focus has been established, the teacher researcher develops a set of personally meaningful questions to guide the inquiry. For example, a teacher might be interested in investigating what happens when students are invited to participate in parent-teacher conferences. Some questions might be: What insights does the student contribute to the conference? How does the parent react to the student's insights? How does the parent react to my interpretation of the student's insights and to my critique of the student's performance? How does the quality of the interaction between the parents and teacher change by having the student participate? How does the student's performance change as a result of participating in the conference?

3. Describing an Intervention:

Sometimes, but not always, teachers may be investigating a specific intervention that is meant to improve whatever the situation might be under study. For example, incorporating student participation into parent-teacher conferences would be the intervention related to the questions above.

4. Collecting Data:

In order to answer the research question(s), the teacher researcher needs to collect valid and reliable data. In action research this is often accomplished by using multiple independent sources of data. Examples of data sources might be found in existing data (school records, including test scores, student work, portfolios); *observational* data (photographs, videotapes, diaries, logs, journals, rating scales, rubrics, data obtained by watching and listening to students throughout the day); and probes (tests, surveys, interviews, focus groups or other means of capturing the voice of others). In one school, a group of teachers involved in various action research projects, agreed that one of their data sources would be their students' voices which they obtained through interviews of individual students, focus groups, and writing prompts.

5. Analyzing Data:

Here is where the *judge* part of our framework comes into play. Reflecting on the data, teacher researchers draw conclusions about what they think the data mean. In this step, teacher researchers search in systematic ways for patterns or trends in the data to assist in answering the following two questions: What is the story told by my data?, and What might explain this story? There are many different ways to analyze data depending on the type of data you collect. This is one area in the process that will require further study on the part of the researcher to determine the most effective and efficient means of making sense out of the data collected. (see "Resources for Further Reflection")

6. Reporting the Findings:

We think this is one of the most interesting, exciting and meaningful parts of the action research process. This is one way of fulfilling one of our professional responsibilities of adding new knowledge to the field. In this step, teachers share their findings with colleagues by writing for publication (consider the NCEA publication *Momentum*), speaking at faculty meetings, brown bag lunches, diocesan workshops, or national conferences (consider submitting a proposal for the NCEA annual convention). Activities such as these really "raise the bar" professionally and certainly speak to our dignity as professionals and the dignity of our work as Catholic educators. In our experience, other teachers are very receptive to hearing the results that fellow teachers have obtained and the teachers who have done the research find this to be a most satisfying experience.

7. Taking Informed Action:

This is really the whole point of conducting action research – planning for students' success based on the information gained from the research process. In this step, teacher researchers engage in action planning, attempting to respond to the question: *"Based on what I have learned from my research, what should I do now?"*

Obviously there is more involved in each of these steps than we have space to discuss here. We have included some resources in the *"Resources for Further Reflection"* section that follows that could help you pursue action research. There might be colleagues within your schools or diocese who have experience conducting research who become resources for you. You might also consider contacting a local university where there may be faculty members who would be very interested in engaging in professional development activities around this topic. Action research is a viable way of engaging in the "observe, judge, act" framework for professional practice we are advocating in this text. Its possibilities for increasing collaboration and dialogue about important issues, improving student performance, re-visioning practice based on new knowledge, developing school-wide priorities, focusing on issues pertinent to Catholic education, and contributing to the profession's body of knowledge about teaching and learning, are endless.

Engaging in Critical Reflection

In Chapters 3 and 4, we raised some challenging and difficult issues based on the assumptions teachers sometimes hold, consciously or not, about the students and families they work with. We tried to highlight some of the effects such assumptions and stereotypes can have on our work with children. These situations typically arise when differences exist between individuals and groups, differences based on gender, class, sexual orientation, race, intellectual ability, and the like. We are certainly not suggesting here that Catholic educators are sexist, racist, homophobic, or anything else. And we are not suggesting that you have not already begun to grapple with these complex issues. Our goal in this short space is to invite you, at whatever place you find yourself, to reflect on these important issues in systematic ways, developing a habit of critical reflection that allows each of us to look inward in order to become more aware of ourselves as cultural beings and the ways culture shape our views about the world.

Let us use a personal example from Mark's experience as a way of showing how this sometimes plays out. For eight years, Mark was the principal of an inner-city Catholic elementary school that was predominantly African-American and low-income. Having come from middle and upper middle class Catholic private schools (both as a student and a professional) he began his tenure believing "kids were kids," not really understanding that race may, in fact, matter. And while he was, at times, concerned that the majority of the teachers in his school were White, and while he and the faculty did make attempts to integrate African-American culture into the school community at many levels, he never really thought deeply about the dynamics of race that were at play in his role as a school administrator.

It was not until further graduate studies, and a particularly provocative course, that he had the opportunity to reflect critically on those eight years, confronting for the first time issues related to his privilege as a White male and his upbringing in a culture and family that was steeped in the racism and classism of the time, and the effect all of this had on his interactions with students, families, and teachers. One point of reflection always comes to mind – after reading and discussing a certain text in a class he was taking, Mark came to the realization that when Black parents accused him of being a racist because of decisions he made, he could, from his privileged position, dismiss the accusations as the reaction of angry, disgruntled parents, rather than address the possibility that his words, actions, or body language may have in fact conveyed his racism. Our reason for sharing a personal story here is that we often do not get the opportunity to reflect at such a critical level and we often do not know how. If it had not been for a particular course with a particular professor who assigned readings that caused serious reflection, and at times resistance, Mark might never have come to some of the realizations he did – what the research would call developing a socio-cultural consciousness (we have included some of this research in the *"Resources for Further Reflection"*).

Knowledge of self and others is the key to this discussion. Developing a socio-cultural consciousness enables teachers to understand that how they perceive the world based on the views they grew up with, is not a universal view, but that it is a view that is greatly impacted by life experiences and their cultural, gender, race, ethnicity, and social class backgrounds. To return to Mark's example for a moment, the fact that he grew up in Detroit and moved to its suburbs as a child in the 1960s and 70s, and that his family had some very definite views on race and ethnicity (a nice way of saying they held some deep prejudices) based on the time and place in which they grew up, clearly impacted his own development as a person and professional. Mark's worldview, like many of our worldviews, was created, in part, by his history and his reaction to that history, which was a very different experience than the students and families he ministered to as principal.

This type of critical reflection is another manifestation of the *"observe, judge, act"* framework we have borrowed from Pope John XXIII. In the process of coming to know ourselves better in this regard, we become aware of the beliefs, values, norms, and practices we ascribe to and which impact our daily lives and our work with students (observe). As we come to realize that our assumptions are socially and personally created based on our historical and cultural context, we make decisions as to their validity and the ways in which they may be affecting our interactions with others, particularly with those who are different from ourselves (judge). The outcome of such a process helps us to see the world differently and as a result we make changes in the ways we think about and interact with others (act). This same process can be used as we come to better know our students and their families. Teachers can become more aware of their students' cultural contexts, family experiences, values and norms through home visits, community study, and family involvement projects that will help to bridge some of the differences that exist between the home and the school. In working through such a process we are striving to become "culturally competent" – knowing oneself and knowing one's students and their families in a way that helps us to interact in well-informed, honest, sincere and genuine ways.

For Catholic educators there is a faith dimension to this process of coming to know oneself and others in this particular way. Understanding ourselves and others is required if we are to answer the call to justice – the call to respect and protect the dignity of each human person we encounter;

the call to build community in solidarity with others for the common good; the call to address needs of all persons, particularly those of the poor and most vulnerable.

We cannot give you a prescription of how to go about this journey. For some of us, it is a very personal journey, while for others it is a journey best made with others. Some of us might just be embarking on such a journey, while others may have already come a long way down this path. It may be a matter of reading some of the excellent literature that is available to challenge our thinking and then using diaries or journals to process our reflections. It may be a matter of taking a course on multicultural education or attending a workshop on diversity. For some, it might be working with a spiritual director and reflecting on scripture and Church documents. Critical reflection is an important disposition for all teachers as it helps us to create new understandings by making conscious our political, social, professional, ethical, and economic assumptions that both constrain and support our work as Catholic educators.

Final Thoughts

It has been a privilege for us to share the voices of the students we interviewed. We have found examining some of the Church's documents on social justice to be a rewarding and challenging academic and faith experience. We hope that by this time you are as excited as we were when we first realized that the children we interviewed were suggesting ideas to us that we had never considered before. It is exciting to see that students want many of the same things that are so important to the Church and to our schools: respect for the individual, a strong sense of community, and equity and justice for all. We have been inspired by these young adolescents to engage in ongoing examination of our practice in order to develop, implement and evaluate our work, with the intention of protecting the dignity of the individual, enhancing community, and ensuring that all student needs are met. We hope that you have been inspired as well to see your work as Catholic educators in new ways, in ways that help to fulfill the Church's important teaching on social justice. We hope you are moved to see anew the profound insights students can share with us about their experiences in our schools as they relate to the justice teaching of the Church. These are times that present unusual challenges to achieving such justice, but we believe that if we implement Pope John XXIII's simple guide to "observe, judge and act," we can respond effectively to the call to justice. As teachers, we can become advocates for justice in our schools, our parishes, our dioceses and in our communities as a whole. We hope that you will engage in ongoing dialogue with us, emailing us with your ideas, challenges and questions (mstorz@jcu.edu or krnestor@mindspring.com.). We hope that your response to the voices you have heard will be another step in your faith journey as Catholic educators who seek to respond to God's for call.

APPENDIX A

Seven Themes of Catholic Social Teaching

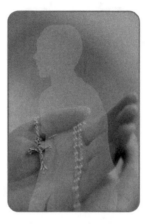

Life and Dignity of the Human Person

The Catholic Church proclaims that human life is sacred and that the dignity of the human person is the foundation of a moral vision for society. Our belief in the sanctity of human life and the inherent dignity of the human person is the foundation of all the principles of our social teaching. In our society, human life is under direct attack from abortion and assisted suicide. The value of human life is being threatened by increasing use of the death penalty. We believe that every person is precious, that people are more important than things, and that the measure of every institution is whether it threatens or enhances the life and dignity of the human person.

Call to Family, Community, and Participation

The person is not only sacred but also social. How we organize our society in economics and politics, in law and policy directly affects human dignity and the capacity of individuals to grow in community. The family is the central social institution that must be supported and strengthened, not undermined. We believe people have a right and a duty to participate in society, seeking together the common good and well-being of all, especially the poor and vulnerable.

Rights and Responsibilities

The Catholic tradition teaches that human dignity can be protected and a healthy community can be achieved only if human rights are protected and responsibilities are met. Therefore, every person has a fundamental right to life and a right to those things required for human decency. Corresponding to these rights are duties and responsibilities to one another, to our families, and to the larger society.

Option for the Poor and Vulnerable

A basic moral test is how our most vulnerable members are faring. In a society marred by deepening divisions between rich and poor, our tradition recalls the story of the Last Judgment (Mt 25:31-46) and instructs us to put the needs of the poor and vulnerable first.

The Dignity of Work and the Rights of Workers

The economy must serve people, not the other way around. Work is more than a way to make a living; it is a form of continuing participation in God's creation. If the dignity of work is to be protected, then the basic rights of workers must be respected the right to productive work, to decent and fair wages, to organize and join unions, to private property, and to economic initiative.

Solidarity

We are our brothers' and sisters' keepers, wherever they live. We are one human family, whatever our national, racial, ethnic, economic, and ideological differences. Learning to practice the virtue of solidarity means learning that "loving our neighbor" has global dimensions in an interdependent world.

Care for God's Creation

We show our respect for the Creator by our stewardship of creation. Care for the earth is not just an Earth Day slogan, it is a requirement of our faith. We are called to protect people and the planet, living our faith in relationship with all of God's creation. This environmental challenge has fundamental moral and ethical dimensions that cannot be ignored.

APPENDIX B

SELECTED QUOTATIONS
From Scripture and Church Documents

What follows are additional scriptural and document references to human dignity, community and preferential option for the poor. These quotations might be helpful in furthering personal and group reflection on these bedrock principles – for personal and/or communal prayer and reflection.

Human Dignity

Scripture

Then some children were brought to Him so that He might lay His hands on them and pray; and the disciples rebuked them. But Jesus said, "Let the children along and do not hinder them from coming to Me; for the kingdom of heaven belongs to such as these. —Matthew 19:13-14

"Truly I say to you, unless you are converted and become like children, you will not enter the kingdom of heaven. Whoever then humbles himself as this child, his is the greatest in the kingdom of heaven. And whoever receives one child, he is the greatest in the kingdom of heaven. And whoever receives one such child in my name receives Me." —Matthew 18:3-5

"What do you think? If any man has a hundred sheep and one of them has gone astray, does he not leave the ninety-nine on the mountains and go and search for the one that is straying? If it turns out that he finds it, truly I say to you, he rejoices over it more than over the ninety-nine which have not gone astray. So it is not the will of your Father who is in heaven that one of these little ones perish. —Matthew 18:12-14

Church Documents

It is furthermore the duty of the State to ensure that terms of employment are regulated in accordance with justice and equity, and to safeguard the human dignity of workers by making sure that they are not required to work in an environment which may prove harmful to their material and spiritual interests. —Mater et Magistra, John XXIII, 1961

Consequently, if the whole structure and organization of an economic system is such as to compromise human dignity, to lessen a man's sense of responsibility or rob him of opportunity for exercising personal initiative, then such a system, We maintain, is altogether unjust – no matter how much wealth it produces, or how justly and equitably such wealth is distributed. —Mater et Magistra, John XXIII, 1961

A civic society is to be considered well ordered, beneficial and in keeping with human dignity if it is grounded on truth. —Pacem in Terris, John XXIII, 1963

Human dignity rests above all on the fact that humanity is called to communion with God. The invitation to converse with God is addressed to men and women as soon as they are born. For if people exist it is because God has created them through love, and through love continues to keep them in existence. They cannot live fully in the truth unless they freely acknowledge that love and entrust themselves to their creator. —Gaudium et Spes, Vatican Council II, 1963

The ferment of the Gospel has aroused and continues to arouse in human hearts an unquenchable thirst for human dignity. —Guadium et Spes, Vatican Council II, 1963

Excessive economic and social disparity between individuals and peoples of the one human race is a source of scandal and militates against social justice, equity, human dignity. —Gaudium et Spes, Vatican Council II, 1963

Behind the facades much misery is hidden, unsuspected even by the closest neighbors; other forms of misery spread where human dignity founders: delinquency, criminality, abuse of drugs and eroticism. —Octogesima Adveniens, Paul VI, 1971

No one can take away this human right, which is based on a commandment; in the words of the Pope: "no man may with impunity violate that human dignity which God himself treats with great reverence," —Centesimus Annus, John Paul II, 1991

Every individual, precisely by reason of the mystery of the Word of God who was made flesh (cf. Jn 1:14), is entrusted to the maternal care of the Church. Therefore every threat to human dignity and life must necessarily be felt in the Church's very heart; it cannot but affect her at the core of her faith in the Redemptive Incarnation of the Son of God, and engage her in her mission of proclaiming the Gospel of life in all the world and to every creature —Evangelium Vitae, John Paul II, 1995

Insisting on the importance and true range of philosophical thought, the Church promotes both the defense of human dignity and the proclamation of the Gospel message. There is today no more urgent preparation for the performance of these tasks than this: to lead people to discover both their capacity to know the truth (124) and their yearning for the ultimate and definitive meaning of life. —Fides et ratio, John Paul II, 1998

Community

Scripture

For just as we have many members in one body and all the members do not have the same function, —Romans 12:4

For even as the body is one and yet has many members, and all the members of the body, though they are many, are one body, so also is Christ. For by one Spirit we were all baptized into one body, whether Jews or Greeks, whether slaves or free, and we were all made to drink of one Spirit. For the body is not one member, but many. —1 Corinthians 12:12-14

But to each one is given the manifestation of the Spirit for the common good. —1 Corinthians 12:7

Do we not all have one father? Has not one God created us? Why do we deal treacherously each against his brother so as to profane the covenant of our fathers? —Malachi 2:10

Church Documents

The common good embraces the sum total of all those conditions of social life which enable individuals, families and organizations to achieve complete and effective fulfillment. —Mater et Magistra, John XXIII, 1961

It is imperative that no one . . . would indulge in a merely individualistic morality. The best way to fulfill one's obligations of justice and love is to contribute to the common good according to one's means and the needs of others, and also to promote and help public and private organizations devoted to bettering the conditions of life. —Gaudium et Spes, Vatican Council II, 1965

The obligation to 'love our neighbor' has an individual dimension, but it also requires a broader social commitment to the common good. —Economic Justice for All, U.S. Catholic Bishops, 1986

Just freedom of action must . . . be left both to individual citizens and to families, yet only on condition that the common good be preserved and wrong to any individual be abolished. The function of the state is to watch over the community and its parts; but in protecting private individuals and rights, chief consideration ought to be given to the weak and the poor. —Centesimus Annus, John Paul II, 1991

The very nature of the common good requires that all members be entitled to share in it, although in different ways according to each one's tasks, merits, and circumstances. —Pacem in Terris, John XXIII, 1963

We have to move from our devotion to independence, through an understanding of interdependence, to a commitment to human solidarity. That challenge must find its realization in the kind of community we build among us. Love implies concern for all – especially the poor – and a continued search for those social and economic structures that permit everyone to share in a community that is a part of a redeemed creation. —Economic Justice for All, U.S. Catholic Bishops, 1986

Catholic social teaching more than anything else insists that we are one family; it calls us to overcome barriers of race, religion, ethnicity, gender, economic status, and nationality. We are all one in Christ Jesus (cf. Gal. 3:28) – beyond our differences and boundaries. —Communities of Salt and Light, U.S. Catholic Bishops, 1993

Yes, human beings are their brother's and sister's keepers. God entrusts us to one another. Our freedom has a relational dimension; we find our fulfillment through the gift of self to others. —Evangelium Vitae, John Paul II, 1995

Preferential Option for the Poor

Scripture

If a man shuts his ears to the cry of the poor, he too will cry out and not be answered. —Proverbs 21:13

You have been a refuge for the poor, a refuge for the needy in his distress, a shelter from the storm and a shade from the heat. For the breath of the ruthless is like a storm driving against a wall. —Isaiah 25:4

But when the Son of Man comes in His glory, and all the angels with Him, then He will sit on His glorious throne. All the nations will be gathered before Him; and He will separate them from one another, as the shepherd separates the sheep from the goats; and He will put the sheep on His right, and the goats on the left. Then the King will say to those on His right, 'Come, you who are blessed of My Father, inherit the kingdom prepared for you from the foundation of the world. For I was hungry, and you gave Me something to eat; I was thirsty, and you gave Me something to drink; I was a stranger, and you invited Me in; naked, and you clothed Me; I was sick, and you visited Me; I was in prison, and you came to Me.' —Matthew 25:31-36

Looking at his disciples, he said: 'Blessed are you who are poor, for yours is the kingdom of God.' —Luke 6:20

Church Documents

Still when there is question of protecting the rights of individuals, the poor and the helpless have a claim to special consideration. —Rerum Novarum, Leo XIII, 1891

The function of the rulers of the State is to watch over the community and its parts; but in protecting private individuals in their rights, chief consideration ought to be given to the weak and the poor. —Quadragesimo Anno, Pius XI, 1931

The joys and the hopes, the griefs and the anxieties of the people of this age, especially those who are poor or in any way afflicted, these are the joys and hopes, the griefs and anxieties of the followers of Christ. —Gaudium et Spes, Second Vatican Council, 1965

The struggle against destitution, though urgent and necessary, is not enough. It is a question, rather, of building a world where every man, no matter what his race, religion or nationality, can live a fully human life, freed from servitude imposed on him by other men or by natural forces over which he has not sufficient control; a world where freedom is not an empty word and where the poor man Lazarus can sit down at the same table with the rich man. This demands great generosity, much sacrifice and unceasing effort on the part of the rich man. —Populorum Progressio, Paul VI, 1967

In teaching us charity, the Gospel instructs us in the preferential respect due the poor and the special situation they have in society: the more fortunate should renounce some of their rights so as to place their goods more generously at the service of others. —Octogesima Adveniens, Paul VI, 1971

Those who are more influential because they have greater share of goods and common services should feel responsible for the weaker and be ready to share with them all they possess . . . the church feels called to take her stand beside the poor, to discern the justice of their requests and to help satisfy them, without losing sight of the good of groups in the context of the common good . . . A consistent theme of Catholic social teaching is the option or love of preference for the poor. Today, this preference has to be expressed in worldwide dimen-

sions, embracing the immense numbers of the hungry, the needy, the homeless, those without medical care, and those without hope. —Solicitudo Rei Socialis, John Paul II, 1987

It is the poor who have a claim to special consideration. The richer class can help itself; the poor have no resources of their own to do so. They chiefly depend on the help of the state. This remains valid today, considering the poverty in the world. —Centesimus Annus, John Paul II, 1991

As individuals and as a nation, therefore, we are called to make a fundamental "option for the poor". The obligation to evaluate social and economic activity from the viewpoint of the poor and the powerless arises from the radical command to love one's neighbor as one's self. Those who are marginalized and whose rights are denied have privileged claims if society is to provide justice for all. This obligation is deeply rooted in Christian belief . . . The obligation to provide justice for all means that the poor have the single most urgent economic claim on the conscience of the nation . . . Decisions must be judged in light of what they do for the poor, what they do to the poor, and what they enable the poor to do for themselves. The fundamental moral criterion for all economic decisions, policies, and institutions is this: They must be at the service of all people, especially the poor —Economic Justice for All, U.S. Catholic Bishops, 1986

The Church's love for the poor . . . is a part of her constant tradition. This love is inspired by the Gospel of the Beatitudes, of the poverty of Jesus, and of his concern for the poor. Love for the poor is even one of the motives for the duty of working so as to be able to give to those in need. —Catechism of the Catholic Church, 2000

RESOURCES FOR FURTHER REFLECTIONS

The following resources are meant to provide opportunities for individuals and groups of teachers to reflect in more depth on some of the topics and issues discussed in the previous chapters. We hope that you will find the variety of resources, Church documents, quotations from scripture and Church documents, websites, and references to a variety of professional articles and books helpful as you delve further into the issues you find most important and most salient in your work as a Catholic educator committed to the social mission of the Church. We have divided this section into (1) resources related Catholic social teaching; (2) educational literature that presents some of the most current research that impacts our work as teachers; and (3) references we cited throughout the chapters. There are obviously many other resources that you might use to further your understanding of Catholic social teaching and best practices; these are some of the ones that we have used in our research and practice and the ones that seem most interesting and provocative in our work as Catholic educators.

Resources related to the Teachings of the Church
Key references to Catholic Social Teaching

Church Documents

Selected papal encyclicals and other Church documents related to the social doctrine of the Church

The following website is an excellent resource for examining major Church documents related to the social mission of the Church: http://www.osjspm.org/cst/doclist.htm. This site includes full text, notable quotations, and summaries of the various documents. Some of the major documents found at this website that we think would be helpful in further studying Catholic social teaching includes:

Rerum Novarum (On the Condition of Labor) —Pope Leo XIII, 1891

Quadragesimo Anno (After Forty Years) —Pope Pius XI, 1931

Mater et Magistra (Mother and Teacher) —Pope John XXIII, 1961

Pacem in Terris (Peace on Earth) —Pope John XXIII, 1963

Gaudium et Spes (Pastoral Constitution on the Church in the Modern World) —Vatican Council II, 1965

Populorum Progressio (On the Development of Peoples) —Pope Paul VI, 1967

Octogesima Adveniens (A Call to Action) —Pope Paul VI, 1971

Justicia in Mundo (Justice in the World) —Synod of Bishops, 1971

Laborem Exercens (On Human Work) —Pope John Paul II, 1981

Solicitudo Rei Socialis (On Social Concern) —Pope John Paul II, 1987

Centesimus Annus (The Hundredth Year) —Pope John Paul II, 1991

Evangelium Vitae (The Gospel of Life) —Pope John Paul II, 1995

Fides et Ratio (Faith and Reason) —Pope John Paul II, 1998

U.S. Bishops Pastoral Letters

Some of the following letters can be found at the above website and at the website of the National Conference of Catholic Bishops website http://www.usccb.org/index.html.

Faithful Citizenship: A Catholic Call to Political Responsibility, 2003

Global Climate Change: A Plea for Dialogue, Prudence, and the Common Good, 2001

Everyday Christianity: To Hunger and Thirst for Justice, 1999

Faithful Citizenship: Political Responsibility for a New Millennium, 1999

The Harvest of Justice is Sown in Peace, 1993

Sharing Catholic Social Teaching: Challenges and Directions, 1999

Brothers and Sisters to Us, 1979

Economic Justice for All, 1986

The Challenge of Peace: God's Promise and our Response, 1983

The Harvest of Justice is Sown in Peace, 1993

Communities of Salt and Light, 1993

The following resources come from various scholars who address Catholic social teaching and were helpful in our preparation of this text:

Cimino, C., Haney, R.M., & O'Keefe, J. (2001). *Integrating the social teaching of the Church into Catholic schools.* Washington D.C.: National Catholic Educational Association.

Fourre, C. (2003). *Journey to justice: Transforming hearts and schools with Catholic social teaching.* Washington, DC: National Catholic Educational Association.

Groome, T. (1998). *Educating for life: A spiritual vision for every teacher and parent.* Thomas More.

Hines, K. R. (2001). *Responses to 101 questions on Catholic social teaching.* New York: Paulist Press.

Kammer, F. (2004). *Doing faithjustice: An introduction to Catholic social thought.* Paulist Press.

Krietemeyer, R. (2000). *Leaven for the modern world: Catholic social teaching and Catholic education.* Washington D.C.: National Catholic Educational Association.

Massaro, T. (2000). *Living justice: Catholic social teaching in action.* Sheed and Ward.

McKenna, K. E. (2002). *A concise guide to Catholic social teaching.* Notre Dame, IN: Ave Maria Press.

Pontifical Council for Justice and Peace. (2004). *Compendium of the social doctrine of the Church.* Washington D.C.: United States Conference of Catholic Bishops.

See also the references listed at the end of the "Resources for Further Reflection" that were cited in the chapters of this text.

Educational Research Literature

The following references are suggested for further scholarly reading in selected areas discussed in previous chapters. What you will find in these references are articles from professional journals and books that address many of the topics and issues we have discussed in this book. You might consider using some of the resources for group study sessions. These are references we have used in our work with pre-service and in-service teachers (or new resources that look worth examining further) which have been very helpful in stimulating discussion and furthering our thinking on these topics. Many may be helpful as you do action planning for your classroom or your school. If you are able to use an electronic data based called ERIC (access through a university or public library or at: www.eric.ed.gov), many of the articles cited below can be downloaded in full text form.

Caring

Collinson, V., Killeavy, M., & Stephenson, H. J. (1999). *Exemplary teachers: Practicing an ethic of care in England, Ireland, and the United States.* Journal for a Just and Caring Education, 5(4), 349-366.

Daniels, D. H., & Perry, K. E. (2003). *"Learner-centered" according to children.* Theory into Practice, 42(2), 102-108.

Lickona, T. (1991). *Educating for character.* New York: Bantam Books.

Lyman, L. (2000). *How do they know you care?* New York: Teachers College Press.

Muller, C., Katz, S. R., & Dance, L. J. (1999). *Investing in teaching and learning: Dynamics of the teacher-student relationship for each actor's perspective.* Urban Education, 34(3), 292-337.

Noddings, N. (2002). *Educating moral people: A caring alternative to character education.* New York: Teachers College Press.

Noddings, N. (1992). *The challenge to care in schools.* New York: Teachers College Press.

High Expectations

Arnold, J. (1997). *High expectations for all: Perspective and practice.* Middle School Journal, 28(3), 51-53.

Clark, L. C. (2002). *Expectations and 'at-risk' children: One teacher's perspective.* In Rethinking our Classrooms, 4(2), 126-128. Milwaukee, WI: Rethinking Schools.

Cotton, K. (2003). *Principals and student achievement: What the research says.* Alexandria VA: Association for Supervision and Curriculum Development.

Landsman, J., & Lewis, C.W. (2006). *White teachers, diverse classrooms: A guide to building inclusive schools, promoting high expectations, and eliminating racism.* Sterling, VA: Stylus Publishers.

Love, A., & Kruger, A.C. (2005). *Teacher beliefs and student achievement in urban schools serving African American students.* Journal of Educational Research, 99(2), 87-99.

Scheideaker, D. (1999). *Bringing out the best in students: How legendary teachers motivate kids.* Thousand Oaks, CA: Corwin Press.

Effective Teaching and Learning Strategies

American Psychological Association. (1997). *Learner-centered psychological principles: A   framework for school redesign and reform.* Retrieved September 15, 2005 from: www.apa.org.

DeVries, R., & Zan, B. (1995). *Creating a constructivist classroom atmosphere.* Young Children, 4-13.

Muir, M. (2001). *What engages underachieving middle school students in learning?* Middle School Journal, 37-43.

Muller, C., Katz, S. R., & Dance, L. J. (1999). *Investing in teaching and learning: Dynamics of the teacher-student relationship for each actor's perspective.* Urban Education, 34(3), 292-337.

Rogat, M. (2004). *Kid to kid: A facilitator's guide to empowering students through open discussions.* Westerville, OH: National Middle School Association.

Teel, K. M., Debruin-Parecki, A., & Covington, M. (1998). *Teaching strategies that honor and motivate inner-city African American students: A school/university collaboration.* Teaching and Teacher Education, 14(5), 479-495.

Tomlinson, C.A. (1999). *The differentiated classroom: Responding to the needs of all learners.* Alexandria, VA: Association for Supervision & Curriculum Development.

Zemelman, S., Daniels, H., & Hyde, A. (1993). *Best practice: New standards for teaching and learning in America's schools.* Portsmouth, NH: Heinemann.

Cultural Issues – Cultural Mismatch

Fordham, S. (1988). *Racelessness as a factor in black students' school success: Pragmatic strategy or pyrrhic victory.* Harvard Educational Review, 58(1), 54-84.

Irvine, J. J. (1990). *Black students and school failure: Policies, practice and prescriptions.* New York: Greenwood Press.

Kaiser, B., & Rasminsky, J. (2003). *Opening the culture door.* Young Children, 58(4), 53-56.

Ogbu, J. (2003). *Black American students in an affluent suburb: A study of academic disengagement.* Mahwah, NJ: Lawrence Earlbaum.

Pransky, K., & Bailey, F. (2002). *To meet your students where they are, first you have to find them: Working with culturally and linguistically diverse at-risk students.* Reading Teacher, 56(4), 370-383.

Parental Involvement

Akers, P. (2005). *Conferencing the SMART Way.* Principal, 84(3), 47.

Booth, A., & Dunn, J. (1996). *Family-school links: How do they affect educational outcomes?* Mahwah, NJ: Lawrence Erlbau.

Boult, B. (2006). *176 ways to involve parents.* Thousand Oaks, CA: Corwin Press.

Epstein, J. L. (2001). *School, family and community partnerships: Preparing educators and improving schools.* Boulder, CO: Westview Press.

Finn, J.D. (1998). *Parent engagement that makes a difference.* Educational Leadership, 55(8), 20-24.

Hampton, F., Mumford, D.A., & Bond, L. (1998). *Parent involvement in inner-city schools: The Project FAST Extended Family Approach to success.* Urban Education, 33(3), 410-427.

Jones, R. (2001). *How parents can support learning: Not all parent involvement programs are equal but research shows what works.* American School Board Journal, 188(9), 18-22.

Ketterer, A. (2003). *Barriers to school involvement and strategies to enhance involvement from parents at a low performing urban school.* Journal of At-Risk Issues, 9(2), 1-7.

Lawrence-Lightfoot, S. (2003) *The essential conversation: What parents and teachers can learn from each other.* New York: Random House.

Lazar, A., & Slostad, F. (1999). *How to overcome obstacles to parent-teacher partnerships.* Clearing House, 72(4), 206-210.

Mierzwik, D. (2004). *Quick and easy ways to connect with students and parents grades K-8: Improving student achievement through parental involvement.* Thousand Oaks, CA: Corwin Press.

Nistler, R. J., & Maiers, A. (2000). *Stopping the silence: Hearing parents' voices in an urban first-grade family literacy program.* The Reading Teacher, 53(8), 670-680.

North Central Regional Educational Laboratory. *Critical Issue: Creating the school climate and structures to support parent and family involvement:* http://www.ncrel.org/sdrs/areas/issues/envrnment/famncomm/pa300.htm. (Note: other resources available on this website).

Swap, S.M. (1993). *Developing home-school partnerships: From concepts to practice.* New York: Teachers College Press.

Culturally-Responsive Teaching

Delpit, L. (1994). *Other people's children: Cultural conflict in the classroom.* New York: New Press.

Gay, G. (2000). *Culturally responsive teaching: Theory, research, and practice.* New York: Teachers College Press.

Howard, T. C. (2001). *Telling their side of the story: African-American students' perceptions of culturally relevant teaching.* The Urban Review, 33(2), 131-140 .

InTime (Integrating New Technologies into the Methods of Education). *Culturally responsive caring:* http://www.intime.uni.edu/multiculture/curriculum/culturecaring.htm.

InTime (Integrating New Technologies into the Methods of Education). *Culturally responsive teaching:* http://www.intime.uni.edu/multiculture.

Irvine, J. J., & Armento, B.J. (2001). *Culturally responsive teaching.* New York: McGraw Hill.

Ladson-Billings, G. (1994). *Dreamkeepers.* San Francisco: Jossey Bass

Lipman, P. (1995). *Bringing out the best in them: The contributions of culturally relevant teachers to educational reform.* Theory into Practice, 34(3), 202-208.

Murell, P. (2002). *African-centered Pedagogy: developing schools of achievement for African-American children.* Albany, NY: State University of New York Press.

Nieto, S. (1999). *The light in their eyes: Creating multicultural learning communities.* New York: Teachers College Press.

Thompson, G., McMillon, P., & Edwards, A. (2000). *Why does Joshua 'hate' school . . . but love Sunday school?* Language Arts, 78(2), 111-120.

Building Community

Friend, M., & Pope, K. L. (2005). *Creating schools in which all students can learn.* Kappa Delta Pi, 41(2), 56-61.

Hoy, W. K., Hannum, J., & Tschannen-Moran, M. (1998). *Organizational climate and student achievement: A parsimonious and longitudinal view.* Journal of School Leadership, 8(4), 336-359.

Marzano, R. J. (2003). *What works in schools: Translating research into action.* Alexandria, VA: Association of Supervision and Curriculum Development.

McLaughlin, M. W., & Talbert, J. (2001). *Professional communities and the work of high school teaching.* Chicago: University of Chicago Press.

Murphy, C. U. (2005). *Whole faculty study groups creating learning communities that target student learning.* Thousand Oaks, CA: Corwin Press.

Responsive Classroom. *Principles and practices:* http://www.responsiveclassroom.org/about/principles.html. (Note: other resources available on this website.)

Richardson, J. (1998). *We're all here to learn.* Journal of Staff Development, 19(4), 49-55.

Supovitz, J. A. (2002). *Developing communities of instructional practice.* Teachers College Record, 104(8), 1591-1626.

Villani, C. (1999). *Community culture and school climate.* School Community Journal, 9(1), 103-105

Examining Assumptions

Downey, D.B., & Pribesh, S. (2004). *When race matters: Teachers' evaluations of students' classroom behavior.* Sociology of Education, 77(4), 267-283.

Howard, T. C. (2003). *Culturally relevant pedagogy: Integrating for critical teacher reflection.* Theory into Practice, 42(3), 195-202.

Johnson, L. (2002). *"My eyes have been opened:" White teachers and racial awareness.* Journal of Teacher Education, 53(2), 153-67.

Milner, H. R. (2003). *Teacher reflection and race in cultural contexts: History, meanings, and methods in teaching.* Theory into Practice, 42(3), 173-180.

Singham, M. (1998). *The canary in the mine: The achievement gap between black and white students.* Phi Delta Kappan, 9-15.

Listening to Students

Cook-Sather, A. (2002). *Authorizing students' perspectives: Toward trust, dialogue, and change in education.* Educational Researcher, 31(4), 3-14.

Kruse, S. (2000). *Student voices: A report from focus group data.* NASSP Bulletin, 84(617), 77-85.

Nieto, S. (1994). *Lessons from students creating a chance to dream.* Harvard Educational Review, 64(4), 392-426.

Waxman, H. C. (1989). *Urban black and Hispanic elementary students' perceptions of classroom instruction.* Journal of Research and Development in Education, 22, 57-61.

Wilson, B. L., & Corbett, H. D. (2001). *Listening to urban kids: School reform and the teachers they want.* Albany, NY: SUNY Press.

Collaboration

Bishop, P., & Allen-Malley, G. (2004). *The power or two: Partner teams in action.* Westerville, OH: National Middle School Association.

Brown, D.F. (2001). *The value of advisory sessions for urban young adolescents.* Middle School Journal, 32(4), 14-22.

Charney, R. S. (2000). *Teaching children to care.* Turner Falls, MA: Northeast Foundation.

Cushman, K (1996). *What does a critical friends group do?* Horace, 13, 1. Available at: http://www.essentialschool,org.

Eaker, R., DuFour, R. and Dufour, R. (2002). *Getting started: Reculturing schools to become professional learning communities.* Bloomington, IN: National Educational Service.

Hord, S.M. (1997). *Professional learning communities: Professional development strategies that improve instruction.* Austin, TX: Southwest Educational Development Laboratory, at: http://www.sedl.org.

James, M., & Spradling, N. (2001). *From advisory to advocacy: Meeting every student's needs.* Westerville, OH: National Middle School Association.

Kriete, R. (2002). *The morning meeting.* Turner Falls, MA: Northeast Foundation.

Responsive Classroom. *Principles and practices:* http://www.responsiveclassroom.org/about/principles.html. (Note: other resources available on this website.)

Rottier, J. (2001). *Implementing and improving teaming: A handbook for middle school teachers.* Westerville, OH: National Middle School Association.

Websites:

Annenberg Institute for School Reform at: http://www.annenberginstitute.org

Coalition of Essential Schools at: http://www.essentialschools.org

National School Reform Faculty at: http://www.nsrfharmony.org

Service Learning

Devine, R., Favazza, J., & McLain, F. (2002). *From cloisters to commons: Concepts and models for service learning in religious studies.* Washington DC: American Association of Higher Education.

England, A., & Spence, J. (1999). *Reflection: A guide to effective service learning.* National Dropout Prevention Center.

Kaye, C. B. (2003). *The complete guide to service learning: Proven, practical ways to engage students in civic responsibility, academic curriculum, and social action.* Free Spirit Publishing.

KIDS Consortium. (2001). *Kids as planners: A guide to strengthening students, schools, and communities through service learning.* Lewiston, ME: KIDS Consortium.

Kielsmeier, J., & Cairn, R. (1991). *Growing hope: A sourcebook on integrating youth service into the school curriculum.* St Paul, MN: National Youth Leadership Council.

Kinsley, C., & McPherson, K. (1995). *Enriching the curriculum through service learning.* Alexandra, VA: Association for Supervision and Curriculum Development.

National Catholic Education Association. (1997). *As we teach we learn.* Washington D.C.: National Catholic Educational Association.

Reidy, P. J. (1997). *To build a civilization of love.* Washington, D.C.: National Catholic Educational Association.

Schine. J. (1997). *Service learning and young adolescent development: A good fit.* In J.L. Irvin (Ed.), What Current Research Says to the Middle Level Practitioner (pp. 257-264). Westerville, OH: National Middle School Association.

Websites:

National Council for the Social Studies: www.socialstudies.org/positions/servicelearning.

National Youth Leadership Council: www.nylc.org.

Developing a Sociocultural Consciousness

Banks, J. (1997). *Educating citizens in a multicultural society.* New York: Teachers College Press.

Harding, S. G. (1991). *Whose science? Whose knowledge? Thinking for women's lives.* Ithaca, NY: Cornell University Press.

Kendall, F. E. (2006). *White privilege: Creating pathways to authentic relationships across race.* New York: Routledge Press.

Tatus, B. (1997). *Why are all the Black kids sitting together in the cafeteria? And other conversations about race.* New York: Basic Books.

Villegas, A. M. & Lucas, T. (2002). *Educating culturally responsive teachers: A coherent approach.* Albany: State University of New Press.

Willis, A. I. & Lewis, K. C. (1998). *Focus on research: A conversation with Gloria Ladson-Billings.* Language Arts, 75(1), 61-70.

Action Research

Arhar, J.M., Holly, M.L., & Kasten, W.C. (2001). *Action research for teachers: Traveling the Yellow Brick Road.* Upper Saddle River, NJ: Merrill Prentice Hall.

Koshy, V. (2005). *Action research for improving practice: A practical guide.* Thousand Oaks, CA: Paul Chapman Publishing.

Mills, G. E. (2000). *Action research: A guide for the teacher researcher.* Upper Saddle River, NJ: Merrill Prentice Hall.

Sagor, R. (2000). *Guiding school improvement with action research.* Alexandria, VA: Association for Supervision and Curriculum Development.

Warrican, S.J. (2006). *Action research: A viable option for effecting change.* Journal of Curriculum Studies, 38(1), 1-14.

References cited in this text

Catholic Church. (2000). *Catechism of the Catholic Church.* Vatican City: Libreria Editrice Vaticana.

Congregation for the Doctrine of the Faith. (1986). *Libertatis Conscientia.*

Curran, C. E. (2002). *Catholic social teaching 1891 – present: A historical, theological, and ethical analysis.* Washington, DC: Georgetown University Press.

DeBerri, E. P., & Hug, J.E. (2003). *Catholic social teaching: Our best kept secret.* Washington DC: Orbis.

Eaker, R., DuFour, R. and Dufour, R. (2002). *Getting started: Reculturing schools to become professional learning communities.* Bloomington, IN: National Educational Service.

Henriot, P. (1997). *Opting for the poor in Catholic education.* Momentum, 28(3), 16-20.

Holy See. (1983). *Charter for the Rights of the Family:* http://www.vatican.va/roman_curia/pontifical_councils/family/documents/rc_pc_family_doc_19831022_family-rights_en.html

Incandela, J. M. (2000). *Education for justice: Stitching a seamless garment.* Horizons, 27(2), 296-310.

John XXIII. (1963). *Pacem in Terris.* http://www.osjspm.org/cst/doclist.htm.

John XXIII. (1961). *Mater et Magistra.* http://www.osjspm.org/cst/doclist.htm.

John Paul II. (1987). *Sollicitudo Rei Socialis.* http://www.osjspm.org/cst/doclist.htm.

John Paul II. (1991). *Centesimus Annus.* http://www.osjspm.org/cst/doclist.htm.

John Paul II. (1992). *Familiaris Consortio:*
http://www.vatican.va/holy_father/john_paul_ii/apost_exhortations/
documents/hf_jp-ii_exh_19811122_familiaris-consortio_en.html.

John Paul II. (1994). *Gratissimam Sane.* http://www.wf-f.org/Letterto
Families.html.

John Paul II. (1995). *Evangelium Vitae.*
http://www.osjspm.org/cst/doclist.htm.

Krietemeyer, R. (2000). *Leaven for the modern world: Catholic social
teaching and Catholic education.* Washington DC: National Catholic
Educational Association. http://www.osjspm.org/cst/doclist.htm.

Lawrence-Lightfoot, S. (2003) *The essential conversation: What parents
and teachers can learn from each other.* New York: Random House.

McDonald, P. (2006). *Annual report on Catholic elementary and
secondary schools.* Washington DC: National Catholic Educational
Association.

National Conference of Catholic Bishops. (1968). *Statement on national
race crisis.* Washington, DC: United States Catholic Conference.

National Conference of Catholic Bishops. (1983). *Challenge of peace:
God's promise, our responsibility.* Washington DC: United States Catholic
Conference.

National Conference of Catholic Bishops. (1986). *Building peace: A pastoral reflection on the response to the challenge of peace.* Washington, DC:
United States Catholic Conference.

National Conference of Catholic Bishops. (1990). *In support of Catholic
elementary and secondary schools.* Washington DC: United States Catholic
Conference.

National Conference of Catholic Bishops. (1993). *Communities of salt and
light.* Washington DC: United States Catholic Conference.

National Conference of Catholic Bishops. (1997). *Renewing the vision: A framework for Catholic youth ministry.* Washington DC: United States Catholic Conference.

National Conference of Catholic Bishops. (1998). *Sharing Catholic social teaching: Challenges and directions.* Washington, DC: United States Catholic Conference.

National Conference of Catholic Bishops. (1998). *Summary of report of the task force on Catholic social teaching and Catholic education.* Washington, DC: United States Catholic Conference.

National Council for the Social Studies. (2000). *Service learning: An essential component of citizenship education.* Available at: http:www.socialstudies.org/positions/servicelearning.

National Leadership Council. (2007). http://www.nylc.org.

Noddings, N. (2005). *"Caring in education,"* in The Encyclopedia of Informal Education, at: http://www.infed.org/biblio/noddings_caring_in_education.htm.

Paul VI. (1971). *Octogesima Adveniens.* http://www.osjspm.org/cst/doclist.htm

Second Vatican Council. (1992). Gaudium et spes. In D. J. O'Brien & T. A. Shannon (Eds.) *Catholic Social thought: The democracy heritage.* Maryknoll, NY: Orbis press.

Synod of Bishops. (1997). *Justicia in Mundo.* http://www.osjspm.org/cst/doclist.htm.

ABOUT THE AUTHORS

Mark G. Storz is currently an associate professor in the Department of Education and Allied Studies at John Carroll University in Cleveland, Ohio, where he directs the teacher preparation programs at the undergraduate and graduate levels. Prior to coming to John Carroll, Mark served as the principal of an urban Catholic elementary school in Flint, Michigan, and as assistant principal and teacher at private Catholic middle/ high schools in Albany and Syracuse, New York. He holds a B.A. in Social Studies Education from Manhattan College, a M.Science in Reading Education from Syracuse University, a M.Arts in Educational Leadership from Eastern Michigan University, and a Ph.D. in Urban Education from Cleveland State University.

Karen R. Nestor has been a Catholic educator for over thirty-five years, as an elementary, middle, and high school teacher, special education tutor, teacher educator, community volunteer, and parent. For the past fifteen years, she has worked as a consultant and coach in urban schools. Currently, she chairs the curriculum development committee for St. Martin de Porres High School, a Cristo Rey school, in Cleveland, Ohio. She is a graduate of Barat College and holds an M.Ed. from Cleveland State University.